SECOND EDITION

PHP Web Services

Lorna Jane Mitchell

Beijing · Boston · Farnham · Sebastopol · Tokyo

PHP Web Services

by Lorna Jane Mitchell

Published by O'Reilly Media, Inc., 1005 Gravenstein Highway North, Sebastopol, CA 95472.

O'Reilly books may be purchased for educational, business, or sales promotional use. Online editions are also available for most titles (*http://safaribooksonline.com*). For more information, contact our corporate/institutional sales department: 800-998-9938 or *corporate@oreilly.com*.

Editor: Allyson MacDonald	**Indexer:** WordCo Indexing Services
Production Editor: Colleen Lobner	**Interior Designer:** David Futato
Copyeditor: Charles Roumeliotis	**Cover Designer:** Randy Comer
Proofreader: James Fraleigh	**Illustrator:** Rebecca Demarest

April 2013:	First Edition
January 2016:	Second Edition

Revision History for the Second Edition

2016-01-05:   First Release

See *http://oreilly.com/catalog/errata.csp?isbn=9781491933091* for release details.

978-1-491-93309-1

[LSI]

Table of Contents

Preface

In this age, when it can sometimes seem like every system is connected to every other system, dealing with data has become a major ingredient in building the Web. Whether you will be delivering services or consuming them, web service is a key part of all modern, public-facing applications, and this book is here to help you navigate your way along the road ahead. We will cover the different styles of service—from RPC, to SOAP, to REST—and you will see how to devise great solutions using these existing approaches, as well as examples of APIs in the wild. Whether you're sharing data between two internal systems, using a service backend for a mobile application, or just plain building an API so that users can access their data, this book has you covered, from the technical sections on HTTP, JSON, and XML to the "big picture" areas such as creating a robust service.

Why did we pick PHP for this book? Well, PHP has always taken on the mission to "solve the web problem." Web services are very much part of that "problem" and PHP is ideally equipped to make your life easy, both when consuming external services and when creating your own. As a language, it runs on many platforms and is the technology behind more than half of the Web, so you can be sure that it will be widely available, wherever you are.

The book walks you through everything you need to know in three broad sections. We begin by covering HTTP and the theory that goes with it, including detailed chapters on the request/response cycle, HTTP verbs and headers, and cookies. There are also chapters on JSON and XML: when to choose each data format, and how to handle them from within PHP. The second section aims to give very practical advice on working with RPC and SOAP services and with RESTful services, and on how to debug almost anything that works over HTTP, using a variety of tools and techniques. In the final section, we look at some of the wider issues surrounding the design of top-quality services, choosing what kind of service will work for your application, and determining how to make it robust. Another chapter is dedicated to handling errors and giving advice on why and how to document your API. Whether you dip into the book as a reference for a specific project, or read it in order to find out more about this area of technology, there's something here to help you and your project find success. Enjoy!

Conventions Used in This Book

The following typographical conventions are used in this book:

Italic

Indicates new terms, URLs, email addresses, filenames, and file extensions.

`Constant width`

Used for program listings, as well as within paragraphs to refer to program elements such as variable or function names, databases, data types, environment variables, statements, and keywords.

`Constant width bold`

Shows commands or other text that should be typed literally by the user.

`Constant width italic`

Shows text that should be replaced with user-supplied values or by values determined by context.

 This element signifies a tip or suggestion.

 This element signifies a general note.

 This element indicates a warning or caution.

Using Code Examples

Supplemental material (code examples, exercises, etc.) is available for download at *https://github.com/lornajane/PHP-Web-Services*.

This book is here to help you get your job done. In general, if this book includes code examples, you may use the code in this book in your programs and documentation. You do not need to contact us for permission unless you're reproducing a significant portion of the code. For example, writing a program that uses several chunks of code from this book does not require permission. Selling or distributing a CD-ROM of examples from O'Reilly books does require permission. Answering a question by citing this book and quoting example code does not require permission. Incorporating a significant amount of example code from this book into your product's documentation does require permission.

We appreciate, but do not require, attribution. An attribution usually includes the title, author, publisher, and ISBN. For example: "*PHP Web Services*, 2nd Edition, by Lorna Jane Mitchell (O'Reilly). Copyright 2016 Lorna Mitchell, 978-1-4919-3309-1."

If you feel your use of code examples falls outside fair use or the permission given above, feel free to contact us at *permissions@oreilly.com*.

Safari® Books Online

 *Safari Books Online* is an on-demand digital library that delivers expert content in both book and video form from the world's leading authors in technology and business.

Technology professionals, software developers, web designers, and business and creative professionals use Safari Books Online as their primary resource for research, problem solving, learning, and certification training.

Safari Books Online offers a range of plans and pricing for enterprise, government, education, and individuals.

Members have access to thousands of books, training videos, and prepublication manuscripts in one fully searchable database from publishers like O'Reilly Media, Prentice Hall Professional, Addison-Wesley Professional, Microsoft Press, Sams, Que, Peachpit Press, Focal Press, Cisco Press, John Wiley & Sons, Syngress, Morgan Kaufmann, IBM Redbooks, Packt, Adobe Press, FT Press, Apress, Manning, New Riders, McGraw-Hill, Jones & Bartlett, Course Technology, and hundreds more. For more information about Safari Books Online, please visit us online.

How to Contact Us

Please address comments and questions concerning this book to the publisher:

O'Reilly Media, Inc.
1005 Gravenstein Highway North
Sebastopol, CA 95472
800-998-9938 (in the United States or Canada)
707-829-0515 (international or local)
707-829-0104 (fax)

We have a web page for this book, where we list errata, examples, and any additional information. You can access this page at *http://bit.ly/php-web-services-2e*.

To comment or ask technical questions about this book, send email to *bookquestions@oreilly.com*.

For more information about our books, courses, conferences, and news, see our website at *http://www.oreilly.com*.

Find us on Facebook: *http://facebook.com/oreilly*

Follow us on Twitter: *http://twitter.com/oreillymedia*

Watch us on YouTube: *http://www.youtube.com/oreillymedia*

Acknowledgments

I'd like to extend my thanks to everyone who made this book happen—from the team at O'Reilly that worked so hard to get the book into its final state, to the technical editors who pointed out howlers and made helpful related suggestions, to various members of the geek community who gave me words of encouragement along the way. Special thanks must go to husband and chief cheerleader Kevin, who has been my biggest supporter all the way through the process.

CHAPTER 1

HTTP

HTTP stands for HyperText Transfer Protocol, and is the basis upon which the Web is built. Each HTTP transaction consists of a *request* and a *response*. The HTTP protocol itself is made up of many pieces: the URL at which the request was directed, the verb that was used, other headers and status codes, and of course, the body of the responses, which is what we usually see when we browse the Web in a browser. We'll see more detailed examples later in the book, but this idea of requests and responses consisting of headers as well as body data is a key concept.

When surfing the Web, ideally we experience a smooth journey between all the various places that we'd like to visit. However, this is in stark contrast to what is happening behind the scenes as we make that journey. As we go along, clicking on links or causing the browser to make requests for us, a series of little "steps" is taking place behind the scenes. Each step is made up of a request/response pair; the client (usually your browser, either on your laptop or your phone) makes a request to the server, and the server processes the request and sends the response back. At every step along the way, the client makes a request and the server sends the response.

As an example, point a browser to *http://lornajane.net* and you'll see a page that looks something like Figure 1-1; either the information desired can be found on the page, or the hyperlinks on that page direct us to journey onward for it.

The web page arrives in the body of the HTTP response, but it tells only half of the story. There is so much more going on in the request and response as they happen; let's inspect that request to *http://lornajane.net* (a pretty average WordPress blog) in more detail.

Request headers:

```
GET / HTTP/1.1
Host: www.lornajane.net
Connection: keep-alive
Cache-Control: no-cache
Accept: text/html,application/xhtml+xml,application/xml;q=0.9,image/webp,*/
*;q=0.8
User-Agent: Mozilla/5.0 (X11; Linux x86_64) AppleWebKit/537.36 (KHTML, like
Gecko) ...
Accept-Encoding: gzip, deflate, sdch
Accept-Language: en-GB,en-US;q=0.8,en;q=0.6
```

Request body: *(no body needed for a GET request)*

Response headers:

```
HTTP/1.1 200 OK
Server: Apache/2.4.7 (Ubuntu)
X-Powered-By: PHP/5.5.9-1ubuntu4.6
X-Pingback: http://www.lornajane.net/xmlrpc.php
Expires: Wed, 11 Jan 1984 05:00:00 GMT
Cache-Control: no-cache, must-revalidate, max-age=0
Content-Encoding: gzip
Content-Type: text/html; charset=UTF-8
Content-Length: 8806
Date: Tue, 15 Sep 2015 08:43:54 GMT
X-Varnish: 612483212
Age: 0
Via: 1.1 varnish
```

Response body (truncated):

```
<!DOCTYPE html>
<head>
<meta charset="UTF-8" />
<meta name="viewport" content="width=device-width" />
<meta name="bitly-verification" content="ff69fb2e45ef"/>
<title>Home - LornaJaneLornaJane | Lorna Jane Mitchell&#039;s Website</title>
<link rel="shortcut icon" href="http://www.lornajane.net/wp-content/themes/lj/
images/favicon.ico">

... (truncated)
```

As you can see, there are plenty of other useful pieces of information being exchanged over HTTP that are not usually seen when using a browser. The browser understands how to work with request and response headers, and handles that so the user doesn't need to.

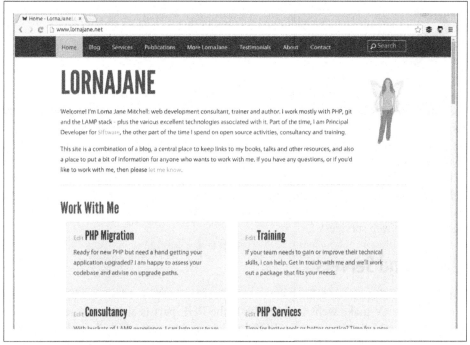

Figure 1-1. Front page of lornajane.net

Understanding this separation between client and server, and the steps taken by the request and response pairs, is key to understanding HTTP and working with web services. Here's an example of what happens when we head to Google in search of kittens:

1. We make a request to *http://www.google.com* and the response contains a `Loca tion` header and a 301 status code sending us to a regional search page; for me that's *http://www.google.co.uk*.

2. The browser follows the redirect instruction (without confirmation from the user; browsers follow redirects by default), makes a request to *http://www.google.co.uk*, and receives the page with the search box (for fun, view the source of this page; there's a lot going on!). We fill in the box and hit search.

3. We make a request to *https://www.google.co.uk/search?q=kittens* (plus a few other parameters) and get a response showing our search results.

The part of the URL after the ? is the "query string" and it's one way of passing additional data to a particular URL or endpoint.

In the story shown here, all the requests were made from the browser in response to a user's actions, although some occur behind the scenes, such as following redirects or requesting additional assets. All the assets for a page, such as images, stylesheets, and so on are fetched using separate requests that are handled by a server. Any content that is loaded asynchronously (by JavaScript, for example) also creates more requests. When we work with APIs, we get closer to the requests and make them in a more deliberate manner, but the mechanisms are the same as those we use to make very basic web pages. If you're already making websites, then you already know all you need to make web services!

Clients and Servers

Earlier in this chapter we talked about a request and response between a client and a server. When we make websites with PHP, the PHP part is always the server. When using APIs, we build the server in PHP, but we can consume APIs from PHP as well. This is the point where things can get confusing. We can create either a client or a server in PHP, and requests and responses can be either incoming or outgoing—or both!

When we build a server, we follow patterns similar to those we use to build web pages. A request arrives, and we use PHP to figure out what was requested and craft the correct response. For example, if we built an API for customers so they could get updates on their orders programmatically, we would be building a server.

Using PHP to consume APIs means we are building a client. Our PHP application makes requests to external services over HTTP, and then uses the responses for its own purposes. An example of a client would be a script that fetches your most recent tweets and displays them.

It isn't unusual for an application to be *both* a client and a server, as shown in Figure 1-2. An application that accepts a request, and then calls out to other services to gather the information it needs to produce the response, is acting as both a client and a server.

When working on applications that are APIs or consume APIs, take care with how you name variables involving the word "request" to avoid confusion!

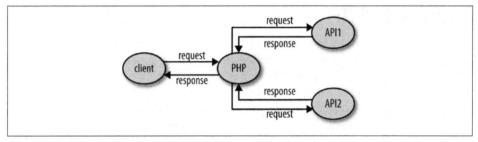

Figure 1-2. Web application acting as a server to the user, but also as a client to access other APIs

Making HTTP Requests

To be able to work with web services, it is important to have a very good understanding of how to work with HTTP from various angles. In this section we'll cover three common ways of working with HTTP:

- Using command-line tools
- Using browser tools
- Using PHP itself

We'll also look at tools specifically designed for inspecting and debugging HTTP in Chapter 10.

The examples here use a site that logs the requests it receives (*http://requestb.in*), which is perfect for exploring how different API requests are seen by a server. To use it, visit the site and create a new "request bin." You will be given a URL to make requests to and be redirected to a page showing the history of requests made to the bin. This is my own favorite tool, not just for teaching HTTP but also when actually building and testing API clients.

There are a few other tools that are similar and could be useful to you when testing. Try out some of these:

- The reserved endpoints (*http://example.com*, *http://example.net*, and *http://example.org*) established by the Internet Assigned Numbers Authority (*http://www.iana.org/domains/special*).
- HTTPResponder (*http://httpresponder.com*) is a similar tool and is on GitHub so you could host/adapt it yourself.
- A selection of endpoints with specific behaviors at httpbin.org.

Register your own endpoint at *http://requestb.in* and use it in place of *http://requestb.in/example* in the examples that follow.

Command-Line HTTP

cURL (*http://curl.haxx.se*) is a command-line tool available on all platforms. It allows us to make any web request imaginable in any form, repeat those requests, and observe in detail exactly what information is exchanged between client and server. In fact, cURL produced the example output at the beginning of this chapter. It is a brilliant, quick tool for inspecting what's going on with a web request, particularly when dealing with something that isn't in a browser or where you need to be more specific about how the request is made. There's also a cURL extension in PHP; we'll cover that shortly in "Doing HTTP with PHP" on page 12, but this section is about the command-line tool.

In its most basic form, a cURL request can be made like this:

```
curl http://requestb.in/example
```

We can control every aspect of the request to send; some of the most commonly used features are outlined here and used throughout this book to illustrate and test the various APIs shown.

If you've built websites before, you'll already know the difference between GET and POST requests from creating web forms. Changing between GET, POST, and other HTTP verbs using cURL is done with the -X switch, so a POST request can be specifically made by using the following:

```
curl -X POST http://requestb.in/example
```

There are also specific switches for GET, POST, and so on, but once you start working with a wider selection of verbs, it's easier to use -X for everything.

To get more information than just the body response, try the -v switch since this will show everything: request headers, response headers, and the response body in full! It splits the response up, though, sending the header information to STDERR and the body to STDOUT:

```
$ curl -v -X POST http://requestb.in/example -d name="Lorna" -d
email="lorna@example.com" -d message="this HTTP stuff is rather excellent"
* Hostname was NOT found in DNS cache
*    Trying 54.197.228.184...
* Connected to requestb.in (54.197.228.184) port 80 (#0)
> POST /example HTTP/1.1
> User-Agent: curl/7.38.0
> Host: requestb.in
> Accept: */*
> Content-Length: 78
> Content-Type: application/x-www-form-urlencoded
>
* upload completely sent off: 78 out of 78 bytes
< HTTP/1.1 200 OK
< Connection: keep-alive
```

```
* Server gunicorn/19.3.0 is not blacklisted
< Server: gunicorn/19.3.0
< Date: Tue, 07 Jul 2015 14:49:57 GMT
< Content-Type: text/html; charset=utf-8
< Content-Length: 2
< Sponsored-By: https://www.runscope.com
< Via: 1.1 vegur
<
* Connection #0 to host requestb.in left intact
```

When the response is fairly large, it can be hard to find a particular piece of information while using cURL. To help with this, it is possible to combine cURL with other tools such as less or grep; however, cURL shows a progress output bar if it realizes it isn't outputting to a terminal, which is confusing to these other tools (and to humans). To silence the progress bar, use the -s switch (but beware that it also silences cURL's errors). It can be helpful to use -s in combination with -v to create output that you can send to a pager such as less in order to examine it in detail, using a command like this:

```
curl -s -v http://requestb.in/example 2>&1 | less
```

The extra 2>&1 is there to send the STDERR output to STDOUT so that you'll see both headers and body; by default, only STDOUT would be visible to less. With the preceding command, you can see the full details of the headers and body, request and response, all available in a pager that allows you to search and page up/down through the output.

Working with the Web in general, and APIs in particular, means working with data. cURL lets us do that in a few different ways. The simplest way is to send data along with a request in key/value pairs—exactly as when a form is submitted on the Web—which uses the -d switch. The switch is used as many times as there are fields to include. To make a POST request as if I had filled in a web form, I can use a curl command like this:

```
curl -X POST http://requestb.in/example -d name="Lorna"
-d email="lorna@example.com"
-d message="this HTTP stuff is rather excellent"
```

APIs accept their data in different formats; sometimes the data cannot be POSTed as a form, but must be created in JSON or XML format, for example. There are dedicated chapters in this book for working with those formats, but in either case we would assemble the data in the correct format and then send it with cURL. We can either send it on the command line by passing a string rather than a key/value pair to a single -d switch, or we can put it into a file and ask cURL to use that file rather than a string (this is a very handy approach for repeat requests where the command line can become very long). If you run the previous request and inspect it, you will see that the body of it is sent as:

```
name=Lorna&email=lorna@example.com
```

We can use this body data as an example of using the contents of a file as the body of a request. Store the data in a file and then give the filename prepended with an @ symbol as a single -d switch to cURL:

```
curl -X POST http://requestb.in/example -d @data.txt
```

Working with the extended features of HTTP requires the ability to work with various headers. cURL allows the sending of any desired header (this is why, from a security standpoint, the header can never be trusted!) by using the -H switch, followed by the full header to send. The command to set the Accept header to ask for an HTML response becomes:

```
curl -H "Accept: text/html" http://requestb.in/example
```

Before moving on from cURL to some other tools, let's take a look at one more feature: how to handle cookies. Cookies will be covered in more detail in Chapter 4, but for now it is important to know that cookies are stored by the client and sent with requests, and that new cookies may be received with each response. Browsers send cookies with requests as default behavior, but in cURL we need to do this manually by asking cURL to store the cookies in a response and then use them on the next request. The file that stores the cookies is called the "cookie jar"; clearly, even HTTP geeks have a sense of humor.

To receive and store cookies from one request:

```
curl -c cookiejar.txt http://requestb.in/example
```

At this point, *cookiejar.txt* contains the cookies that were returned in the response. The file is a plain-text file, and the way that a browser would store this information is pretty similar; the data is just text. Feel free to open this file in your favorite text editor; it can be amended in any way you see fit (which is another good reminder of why trusting outside information is a bad idea; it may well have been changed), and then sent to the server with the next request you make. To send the cookie jar, amended or otherwise, use the -b switch and specify the file to find the cookies in:

```
curl -b cookiejar.txt http://requestb.in/example
```

To capture cookies and resend them with each request, use both the -b and -c switches, referring to the same *cookiejar* file with each switch. This way, all incoming cookies are captured and sent to a file, and then sent back to the server on any subsequent request, behaving just as they do in a browser. This approach is useful if you want to test something from cURL that requires, for example, logging in.

Another command-line tool well worth a mention here is HTTPie (*http://httpie.org*), which claims to be a cURL-like tool for humans. It has many nice touches that you may find useful, such as syntax highlighting. Let's see some examples of the same kinds of requests that we did with cURL.

The first thing you will probably notice (for example, in Figure 1-3) is that HTTPie gives more output.

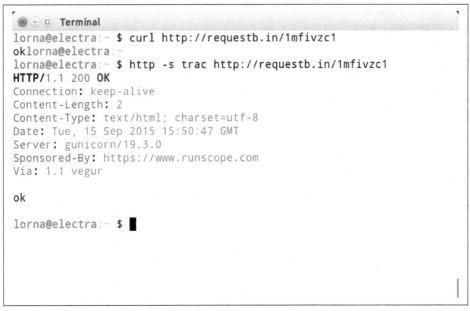

Figure 1-3. A simple GET request with both cURL and HTTPie

You can control what HTTPie outputs with the `--print` or `-p` switch, and pass H to see the request header, B to see the request body, h to see the response header, or b to see the response body. These can be combined in any way you like and the default is hb. To get the same output as cURL gives by default, use the b switch:

```
http -p b http://requestb.in/example
```

HTTPie will attempt to guess whether each additional item after the URL is a form field, a header, or something else. This can be confusing, but once you've become used to it, it's very quick to work with. Here's an example with POSTing data as if submitting a form:

```
$ http -p bhBH -f http://requestb.in/example name=Lorna email=lorna@example.com
message="This HTTP stuff is rather excellent"

POST /example HTTP/1.1
Accept: */*
Accept-Encoding: gzip, deflate
Connection: keep-alive
Content-Length: 80
Content-Type: application/x-www-form-urlencoded; charset=utf-8
Host: requestb.in
User-Agent: HTTPie/0.8.0
```

```
name=Lorna&email=lorna%40example.com&message=This+HTTP+stuff+is+rather+excellent

HTTP/1.1 200 OK
Connection: keep-alive
Content-Length: 2
Content-Type: text/html; charset=utf-8
Date: Tue, 07 Jul 2015 14:46:28 GMT
Server: gunicorn/19.3.0
Sponsored-By: https://www.runscope.com
Via: 1.1 vegur

ok
```

To add a header, the approach is similar; HTTPie sees the : in the argument and uses it as a header. For example, to send an Accept header:

```
$ http -p H -f http://requestb.in/example Accept:text/html

GET /149njzd1 HTTP/1.1
Accept: text/html
Accept-Encoding: gzip, deflate
Connection: keep-alive
Content-Type: application/x-www-form-urlencoded; charset=utf-8
Host: requestb.in
User-Agent: HTTPie/0.8.0
```

Whether you choose cURL or HTTPie is a matter of taste; they are both worth a try and are useful tools to have in your arsenal when working with HTTP.

Browser Tools

All the newest versions of the modern browsers (Chrome, Firefox, Opera, Safari, Internet Explorer) have built-in tools or available plug-ins to help inspect the HTTP that's being transferred, and for simple services you may find that your browser's tools are an approachable way to work with an API. These tools vary between browsers and are constantly updating, but here are a few favorites to give you an idea.

In Firefox, this functionality is provided by the Developer Toolbar and various plug-ins. Many web developers are familiar with FireBug (*http://getfirebug.com*), which does have some helpful tools, but there is another tool that is built specifically to show you all the headers for all the requests made by your browser: LiveHTTPHeaders (*http://livehttpheaders.mozdev.org*). Using this, we can observe the full details of each request, as seen in Figure 1-4.

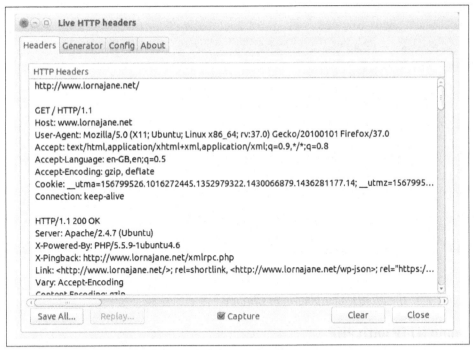

Figure 1-4. LiveHTTPHeaders showing HTTP details

All browsers offer some way to inspect and change the cookies being used for requests to a particular site. In Chrome, for example, this functionality is offered by an extension called "Edit This Cookie," and other similar extentions. This shows existing cookies and lets you edit and delete them—and also allows you to add new cookies. Take a look at the tools in your favorite browser and see the cookies sent by the sites you visit the most.

Sometimes, additional headers need to be added to a request, such as when sending authentication headers, or specific headers to indicate to the service that we want some extra debugging. Often, cURL is the right tool for this job, but it's also possible to add the headers into your browser. Different browsers have different tools, but for Chrome try an extension called ModHeader, seen in Figure 1-5.

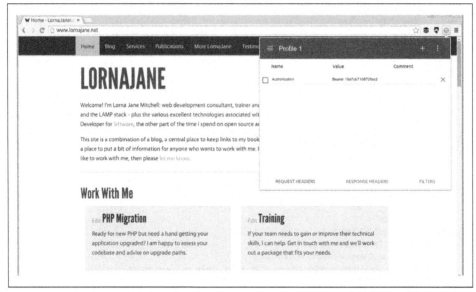

Figure 1-5. The ModHeader plug-in in Chrome

Doing HTTP with PHP

You won't be surprised to hear that there is more than one way to handle HTTP requests using PHP, and each of the frameworks will also offer their own additions. This section focuses on plain PHP and looks at three different ways to work with APIs:

- PHP's cURL extension (usually available in PHP, sometimes via an additional package)
- PHP's built-in stream-handling functionaltiy
- Guzzle (a PHP library)

Earlier in this chapter, we discussed a command-line tool called cURL (see "Command-Line HTTP" on page 6). PHP has its own wrappers for cURL, so we can use the same tool from within PHP. A simple GET request looks like this:

```php
<?php

$url = "http://www.lornajane.net/";
$ch = curl_init($url);

curl_setopt($ch, CURLOPT_RETURNTRANSFER, true);
$result = curl_exec($ch);
curl_close($ch);
```

The previous example is the simplest form; it sets the URL, makes a request to its location (by default this is a GET request), and capture the output. Notice the use of curl_setopt(); this function is used to set many different options on cURL handles and it has excellent and comprehensive documentation on *http://php.net*. In this example, it is used to set the CURLOPT_RETURNTRANSFER option to true, which causes cURL to *return* the results of the HTTP request rather than *output* them. There aren't many use cases where you'd want to output the response so this flag is very useful.

We can use this extension to make all kinds of HTTP requests, including sending custom headers, sending body data, and using different verbs to make our request. Take a look at this example, which sends some JSON data and a Content-Type header with the POST request:

```php
<?php

$url = "http://requestb.in/example";
$data = ["name" => "Lorna", "email" => "lorna@example.com"];

$ch = curl_init($url);
curl_setopt($ch, CURLOPT_POST, 1);
curl_setopt($ch, CURLOPT_POSTFIELDS, json_encode($data));

curl_setopt($ch, CURLOPT_HTTPHEADER,
    ['Content-Type: application/json']
);
curl_setopt($ch, CURLOPT_RETURNTRANSFER, true);
$result = curl_exec($ch);
curl_close($ch);
```

Again, curl_setopt() is used to control the various aspects of the request we send. Here, a POST request is made by setting the CURLOPT_POST option to 1, and passing the data we want to send as an array to the CURLOPT_POSTFIELDS option. We also set a Content-Type header, which indicates to the server what format the body data is in; the various headers are covered in more detail in Chapter 3.

The PHP cURL extension isn't the easiest interface to use, although it does have the advantage of being reliably available. Another great way of making HTTP requests that is always available in PHP is to use PHP's stream-handling abilities with the file functions. In its simplest form, this means that, if allow_url_fopen is enabled (see the PHP manual (*http://bit.ly/php-allow_url_fopen*)), it is possible to make requests using file_get_contents(). The simplest example is making a GET request and reading the response body in as if it were a local file:

```php
<?php

$result = file_get_contents("http://www.lornajane.net/");
```

We can take advantage of the fact that PHP can handle a variety of different protocols (HTTP, FTP, SSL, and more) and files using streams. The simple GET requests are easy, but what about something more complicated? Here is an example that makes the same POST request as our earlier example with JSON data and headers, illustrating how to use various aspects of the streams functionality:

```php
<?php

$url = "http://requestb.in/example";
$data = ["name" => "Lorna", "email" => "lorna@example.com"];

$context = stream_context_create([
    'http' => [
        'method' => 'POST',
        'header' => ['Accept: application/json',
            'Content-Type: application/json'),
        'content' => json_encode($data)
    ]
]);

$result = file_get_contents($url, false, $context);
```

Options are set as part of the *context* that we create to dictate how the request should work. Then, when PHP opens the stream, it uses the information supplied to determine how to handle the stream correctly—including sending the given data and setting the correct headers.

The third way that I'll cover here for working with PHP and HTTP is Guzzle (*http://guzzlephp.org*), a PHP library that you can include in your own projects with excellent HTTP-handling functionality. It's installable via Composer (*http://getcomposer.org*), or you can download the code from GitHub and include it in your own project manually if you're not using Composer yet (the examples here are for version 6 of Guzzle).

For completeness, let's include an example of making the same POST request as before, but this time using Guzzle:

```php
<?php

require "vendor/autoload.php";

$url = "http://requestb.in/example";
$data = ["name" => "Lorna", "email" => "lorna@example.com"];

$client = new \GuzzleHttp\Client();

$result = $client->post($url, ["json" => $data]);
echo $result->getBody();
```

The Guzzle library is object-oriented and it has excellent documentation (*http://docs.guzzlephp.org*), so do feel free to take these examples and build on them using the documentation for reference. The preceding example first includes the Composer autoloader since that's how I installed Guzzle. Then it initializes both the URL that the request will go to and the data that will be sent. Before making a request in Guzzle, a client is initialized, and at this point you can set all kinds of configuration on either the client to apply to all requests, or on individual requests before sending them. Here we're simply sending a POST request and using the json config shortcut so that Guzzle will encode the JSON and set the correct headers for us. You can see this in action by running this example and then visiting your *http://requestb.in* page to inspect how the request looked when it arrived.

As you can see, there are a few different options for dealing with HTTP, both from PHP and the command line, and you'll see all of them used throughout this book. These approaches are all aimed at "vanilla" PHP, but if you're working with a framework, it will likely offer some functionality along the same lines; all the frameworks will be wrapping one of these methods so it will be useful to have a good grasp of what is happening underneath the wrappings. After trying out the various examples, it's common to pick one that you will work with more than the others; they can all do the job, so the one you pick is a result of both personal preference and which tools are available (or can be made available) on your platform. Most of my own projects make use of streams unless I need to do something nontrivial, in which case I use Guzzle as it's so configurable that it's easy to build up all the various pieces of the request and still understand what the code does when you come back to it later.

CHAPTER 2

HTTP Verbs

HTTP verbs such as GET and POST let us send our intention along with the URL so we can instruct the server what to do with it. Web requests are more than just a series of addresses, and verbs contribute to the rich fabric of the journey. This chapter covers how to make and respond to HTTP requests using a selection of common HTTP verbs, including lots of examples.

I mentioned GET and POST because it's very likely you're already familiar with those. There are many verbs that *can* be used with HTTP—in fact, we can even invent our own—but we'll get to that later in the chapter (see "Using Other HTTP Verbs" on page 23). First, let's revisit GET and POST in some detail, looking at when to use each one and what the differences are between them.

Serving GET Requests

URLs used with GET can be bookmarked, they can be called as many times as needed, and the request should change the data it accesses. A great example of using a GET request when filling in a web form is when using a search form, which should always use GET. Searches can be repeated safely, and the URLs can be shared.

Consider the simple web form in Figure 2-1, which allows users to state which category of results they'd like and how many results to show. The code for displaying the form and the (placeholder) search results on the page could be something like this:

```
<html>
<head>
<title>GET Form</title>
<link rel="stylesheet" href="http://yui.yahooapis.com/pure/0.6.0/pure-min.css">
</head>
<body>
<div style="margin: 20px">
```

```
<h1>A GET Form</h1>

<?php if(empty($_GET)): ?>

<form name="search" method="get" class="pure-form pure-form-stacked">
    Category:
    <select name="category">
        <option value="entertainment">Entertainment</option>
        <option value="sport">Sport</option>
        <option value="technology">Technology</option>
    </select>

    Rows per page: <select name="rows">
        <option value="10">10</option>
        <option value="20">20</option>
        <option value="50">50</option>
    </select>

    <input type="submit" value="Search" class="pure-button pure-button-
primary"/>
</form>

<?php else: ?>

<p>Wonderfully filtered search results</p>

<?php endif; ?>

</div>
</body>
</html>
```

You can see that PHP simply checks if it has been given some search criteria (or indeed any data in the $_GET superglobal) and if not, it displays the empty form. If there was data, then it would process it (although probably in a more interesting way than this trivial example does). The data gets submitted on the URL when the form is filled in (GET requests typically have no body data), resulting in a URL like this:

http://localhost/book/get-form-page.php?category=technology&rows=20

Having the data visible on the URL is a design choice. When this happens, a user can easily bookmark or share this URL with others, which is sometimes very useful, for example, to bookmark a particular set of search results, or a product page. In other use cases, such as submitting a form to update a user's profile, we really don't want users to be able to share or save the request that they made, so a POST request would be more appropriate. As software developers, we need to choose whether to submit forms via GET or POST, and in general a good rule of thumb is that if the request is safe to repeat, then GET is a good choice; otherwise use POST. We'll see more examples of the correct use of verbs in APIs as well as forms during this chapter.

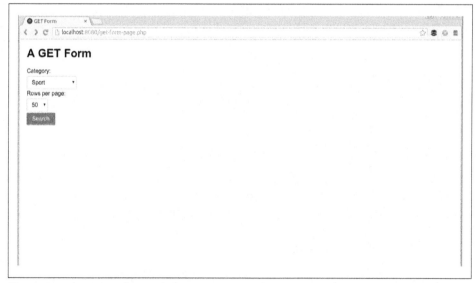

Figure 2-1. An example search form

Making GET Requests

The previous example showed how PHP responds to a GET request, but how does it make one? Well, as discussed in Chapter 1, there are many ways to approach this. For a very quick solution, use PHP's stream handling to create the complete request to send:

```php
<?php

$url = 'http://localhost/book/get-form-page.php';
$data = ["category" => "technology", "rows" => 20];

$get_addr = $url . '?' . http_build_query($data);
$page = file_get_contents($get_addr);
echo $page;
```

In a Real World™ system, it is prudent to be cautious of the data coming in from external APIs; it is best to filter the contents of $page before outputting it or using it anywhere else. As an alternative to using PHP's stream features, you could use whatever functionality your existing frameworks or libraries offer, or make use of the cURL extension that is built in to PHP.

Using cURL, our code would instead look like this:

```php
<?php

$url = 'http://localhost/book/get-form-page.php';
$data = ["category" => "technology", "rows" => 20];

$get_addr = $url . '?' . http_build_query($data);
$ch = curl_init($get_addr);
curl_setopt($ch, CURLOPT_RETURNTRANSFER, 1);
$page = curl_exec($ch);
echo $page;
```

Either of these approaches works well when you want to fetch data into your PHP script from an external API or page. The examples here show web pages, but they apply when working with HTML, XML, JSON, or anything else.

Handling POST Requests

In contrast to GET requests, a POST request is one that does cause change on the server that handles the request. These requests shouldn't be repeated or bookmarked, which is why your browser warns you when it is resubmitting data. Let's use a POST form when the request changes data on the server side. Figure 2-2, for example, involves updating a bit of user profile information.

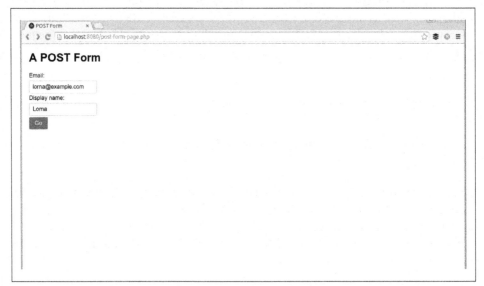

Figure 2-2. Simple form that updates data, sending content via a POST request

When a form is submitted via GET, we can see the variables being sent on the URL. With POST, however, the data goes into the *body* of the request, and the Content-Type header denotes what kind of data can be found in the body. When we fill in the form in Figure 2-2, the request looks like this:

```
POST /book/post-form-page.php HTTP/1.1
Host: localhost
Content-Length: 48
Accept: text/html,application/xhtml+xml,application/xml;q=0.9,*/*;q=0.8
Content-Type: application/x-www-form-urlencoded
Accept-Encoding: gzip,deflate,sdch
Accept-Language: en-GB,en-US;q=0.8,en;q=0.6
Accept-Charset: ISO-8859-1,utf-8;q=0.7,*;q=0.3

email=lorna%40example.com&display_name=LornaJane
```

In this example, you can see the data in the body, with the `Content-Type` and `Content-Length` headers set appropriately so that the server can decode the response (more about content negotiation in Chapter 3). Next we'll look at the server side of the conversation.

PHP knows how to handle form data, so it can parse this out and place the fields into `$_POST`, so it will be ready for use in the script. Here is the code behind this page, showing the form without any incoming data; if data existed, it would be displayed:

```html
<html>
<head>
<title>POST Form</title>
<link rel="stylesheet" href="http://yui.yahooapis.com/pure/0.6.0/pure-min.css">
</head>
<body>
<div style="margin: 20px">
<h1>A POST Form</h1>

<?php if(empty($_POST)): ?>

<form name="user" method="post" class="pure-form pure-form-stacked">
    Email:
    <input type="text" length="60" name="email" />

    Display name:
    <input type="text" length="60" name="display_name" />

    <input type="submit" value="Go" class="pure-button pure-button-primary"/>
</form>

<?php else:
    echo "New user email: " . filter_input(INPUT_POST,
        "email", FILTER_VALIDATE_EMAIL);
endif; ?>

</div>
</body>
</html>
```

It is very common to build PHP forms and parse data in this way, but when handling HTTP requests, it is also important to consider how the requests can be made and responded to (spoiler: it looks a lot like our GET request code).

Making POST Requests

To POST data to this form using streams (as in "Making GET Requests" on page 19), the same basic approach can be used, but some *context* should be added to the stream, so it will know which methods, headers, and verbs to use:

```php
<?php

$url = 'http://localhost/book/post-form-page.php';
$data = ["email" => "lorna@example.com", "display_name" => "LornaJane"];
$options = ["http" =>
    ["method"  => "POST",
        "header"  => "Content-Type: application/x-www-form-urlencoded",
        "content" => http_build_query($data)
    ]
];

$page = file_get_contents($url, NULL, stream_context_create($options));
echo $page;
```

When POST data is sent to the page created, the data sent appears in the output rather than in the form, so it shows "New user email: *lorna@example.com*." This code looks very similar to the previous streams example, but this example uses stream_con text_create() to add some additional information to the stream.

You can see that we added the body content as a simple string, formatted it as a URL using http_build_query(), and indicated which content type the body is. This means that other data formats can very easily be sent by formatting the strings correctly and setting the headers.

Here is an example that makes the same POST request again, but this time using Guzzle (these examples are for version 6 of Guzzle):

```php
<?php
require "vendor/autoload.php";

$url = 'http://localhost/book/post-form-page.php';
$data = ["email" => "lorna@example.com", "display_name" => "LornaJane"];

$client = new \GuzzleHttp\Client();
$page = $client->post($url, ["form_params" => $data]);
echo $page->getBody();
```

This looks very similar to the previous example, but using the built-in form_params option to Guzzle means that the Content-Type will be specified for us (there is also a multipart option if you need to send file uploads using Guzzle). When we make the request, we get a response object back rather than a string, but we can access the content using the getBody() method.

 In these simple examples, we can make our code make POST requests to HTML forms because the forms have no security features. In reality, most forms will have some CSRF (Cross-Site Request Forgery) protection in them, so you'll find that you usually can't make requests like this against forms published on the wider Internet. I would always recommend that you include security features in your own forms—except when you're trying out the previous examples, of course.

Using Other HTTP Verbs

There are many specifications relating to HTTP, as well as protocols based upon it, and between them they define a wide selection of verbs that can be used with HTTP. Even better, there is always room to invent new HTTP verbs; so long as your client and server both know how to handle a new verb, it is valid to use it. However, be aware that not all elements of network infrastructure between these two points will necessarily know how to handle every verb. Some pieces of network infrastructure do not support PATCH, for example, or the verbs used by the WebDAV protocol. When working with APIs, particularly RESTful ones, it is normal to make use of two additional verbs: PUT and DELETE. REST is covered in detail in Chapter 8, but for now it is useful to examine some examples of how to use these less common verbs in applications.

The simplest of these two is DELETE, because it doesn't have any body data associated with it. It is possible to see what kind of request was made to a PHP script acting as a server by inspecting the $_SERVER["REQUEST_METHOD"] value, which indicates which verb was used in the request.

To make the request from PHP, it is necessary to set the verb and then make the request as normal. Here's an example using the cURL extension:

```php
<?php

$url = 'http://localhost/book/example-delete.php';

$ch = curl_init($url);
curl_setopt($ch, CURLOPT_CUSTOMREQUEST, "DELETE");
curl_exec($ch);
```

This example simply issues a request to the $url shown using a DELETE verb.

Using PUT is slightly more involved because, like POST, it can be accompanied by data and the data can be in a variety of formats. In "Handling POST Requests" on page 20, I mentioned that for incoming form data, PHP reads form-encoded values for POST and creates a $_POST array for us. There is no equivalent $_PUT superglobal, but we can still make use of the *php://input* stream to inspect the body data of the request to which the script is sending a response at that time.

When using PHP to respond to PUT requests, the code runs along the lines of this example:

```php
<?php

if($_SERVER['REQUEST_METHOD'] == "PUT") {
    $data = [];
    $incoming = file_get_contents("php://input");
    parse_str($incoming, $data);
    echo "New user email: " . filter_var($data["email"], FILTER_VALIDATE_EMAIL);
} else {
    echo "The request did not use a PUT method";
}
```

This example inspects the $_SERVER superglobal to see which verb was used, and then responds accordingly. The data coming into this example is form style, meaning it uses file_get_contents() to grab all the body data, then parse_str() to decode it.

 Be careful with parse_str()—if the second argument is omitted, the variables will be extracted as local variables, rather than contained in an array.

In order to use PHP to make a request that the previous script can handle, it is necessary to create the contents of the body of the request and specify that it is a PUT request. Below is an example using the Guzzle library:

```php
<?php

require "vendor/autoload.php";

$url = "http://localhost/book/put-form-page.php";
$data = ["email" => "lorna@example.com", "display_name" => "LornaJane"];

$client = new \GuzzleHttp\Client();
$result = $client->put($url, [
    "headers" => ["Content-Type" => "application/x-www-form-urlencoded"],
    "body" => http_build_query($data)
]);

echo $result->getBody();
```

The PUT verb is specified in this example, and the correct header for the form-encoded data is set. We dictate the data to PUT (manually building the form elements into a string) and then send the request. We will discuss more about other data formats in Chapter 5 and Chapter 6, which cover JSON and XML specifically, but the basic principles of preparing the data and setting the Content-Type header accordingly still stand.

Armed with this knowledge of how to handle GET, POST, DELETE, and PUT verbs, we are able to work with many different kinds of API acting as both a client and as a server. When using other verbs, either those that already exist as part of the HTTP spec or those that are custom to your application, you can use the approaches described here for PUT and DELETE.

CHAPTER 3

Headers

So far, we've seen various presentations of the HTTP format, and examined the idea that there is a lot more information being transferred in web requests and responses than what appears in the body of the response. The body is certainly the most important bit, and often is the meatiest, but the headers provide key pieces of information for both requests and responses, which allow the client and the server to communicate effectively. If you think of the body of the request as a birthday card with a check inside it, then the headers are the address, postmark, and perhaps the "do not open until…" instruction on the outside (see Figure 3-1).

Figure 3-1. Envelope with stamp, address, and postmark

This additional information gets the body data to where it needs to go and instructs the target on what to do with it when it gets there.

Request and Response Headers

Many of the headers you see in HTTP make sense in both requests and responses. Others might be specific to *either* a request *or* a response. Here's a sample set of real request and response headers from when I request my own site (*http://www.lorna jane.net*) from a browser (I'm using Chrome).

Request headers:

```
GET / HTTP/1.1
Host: www.lornajane.net
Connection: keep-alive
Accept: text/html,application/xhtml+xml,application/xml;q=0.9,image/webp,*/
*;q=0.8
User-Agent: Mozilla/5.0 (X11; Linux x86_64) AppleWebKit/537.36 (KHTML, like
Gecko) Chrome/43.0.2357.81 Safari/537.36
Accept-Encoding: gzip, deflate, sdch
Accept-Language: en-GB,en-US;q=0.8,en;q=0.6
Accept-Charset: ISO-8859-1,utf-8;q=0.7,*;q=0.3
```

Response headers:

```
HTTP/1.1 200 OK
Server: Apache/2.4.7 (Ubuntu)
X-Powered-By: PHP/5.5.9-1ubuntu4.6
X-Pingback: http://www.lornajane.net/xmlrpc.php
Expires: Wed, 11 Jan 1984 05:00:00 GMT
Cache-Control: no-cache, must-revalidate, max-age=0
Vary: Accept-Encoding
Content-Encoding: gzip
Content-Type: text/html; charset=UTF-8
Content-Length: 7897
Accept-Ranges: bytes
Date: Sat, 11 Jul 2015 08:22:57 GMT
X-Varnish: 600223060
Age: 0
Via: 1.1 varnish
Connection: keep-alive
```

Headers can be related to the request, the response, or the "entity," which is the body of either a request or a response. Some examples might be:

Request Headers   User-Agent, Accept, Authorization, and Cookie

Response Headers   Set-Cookie

Entity Headers   Content-Type and Content-Length

This chapter looks in more detail at the headers you are likely to see when working with web services.

Identify Clients with User-Agent

The User-Agent header gives information about the client making the HTTP request and usually includes information about the software client. Take a look at the header here:

```
User-Agent Mozilla/5.0 (Linux; U; Android 2.3.4; en-gb; SonyEricssonSK17i Build/
4.0.2.A.0.62) AppleWebKit/533.1 (KHTML, like Gecko) Version/4.0 Mobile Safari/
533.1
```

What device do you think made this request? You would probably guess that it was my Sony Ericsson Android phone...and perhaps you would be right. Or perhaps I used a curl command:

```
curl -H "User-Agent: Mozilla/5.0 (Linux; U; Android 2.3.4; en-gb; SonyErics-
sonSK17i Build/4.0.2.A.0.62) AppleWebKit/533.1 (KHTML, like Gecko) Version/4.0
Mobile Safari/533.1" http://requestb.in/example
```

We simply have no way of knowing, when a request is received with a User-Agent like this, if it *really* came from an Android phone, or if it came from something else *pretending* to be an Android phone. This information can be used to customize the response we send—after all, if someone wants to pretend to be a tiny Android phone, then it is reasonable to respond with the content that would normally be sent to this phone. It does mean, however, that the User-Agent header cannot be relied upon for anything more important, such as setting a custom header and using it as a means of authenticating users. Just like any other incoming data, it is wide open to abuse and must be treated with suspicion.

In PHP, it is possible both to parse and to send the User-Agent header, as suits the task at hand. Here's an example of sending the header using streams:

```php
<?php

$url = 'http://localhost/book/user-agent.php';
$options = array(
    "http" => array(
        "header"  => "User-Agent: Advanced HTTP Magic Client"
    )
);

$page = file_get_contents($url, false , stream_context_create($options));
echo $page;
```

We can set any arbitrary headers we desire when making requests, all using the same approach. Similarly, headers can be retrieved using PHP by implementing the same approach throughout. The data of interest here can all be found in $_SERVER, and in this case it is possible to inspect $_SERVER["HTTP_USER_AGENT"] to see what the User-Agent header was set to.

To illustrate, here's a simple script:

```php
<?php

echo "This request made by: "
    . filter_var($_SERVER['HTTP_USER_AGENT'], FILTER_SANITIZE_STRING);
```

It's common when developing content for the mobile web to use headers such as User-Agent in combination with WURFL (*http://wurfl.sourceforge.net/*) to detect what capabilities the consuming device has, and adapt the content accordingly. With APIs, however, it is better to expect the clients to use other headers so they can take responsibility for requesting the correct content types, rather than allowing the decision to be made centrally.

Headers for Content Negotiation

Commonly, the Content-Type header is used to describe what format the data being delivered in the body of a request or a response is in; this allows the target to understand how to decode this content. Its sister header, Accept, allows the client to indicate what kind of content is *acceptable*, which is another way of allowing the client to specify what kind of content it actually knows how to handle. As seen in the earlier example showing headers, here's the Accept header Google Chrome usually sends:

```
Accept: text/html,application/xhtml+xml,application/xml;q=0.9,image/webp,
*/*;q=0.8
```

To read an Accept header, consider each of the comma-separated values as an individual entity. This client has stated a preference for (in order):

- text/html
- application/xhtml+xml
- image/webp
- application/xml
- */*

This means that if any of these formats are supplied, the client will understand our meaning. There are two entries in the list that include some additional information: the q value. This is an indication of how much a particular option is preferred, where the default value is q=1.

Here, Chrome claims to be able to handle a content type of */*. The asterisks are wildcards, meaning it thinks it can handle any format that could possibly exist—which seems unlikely. If an imaginary format is implemented that both our client and server understand, for example, Chrome won't know how to parse it, so */* is misleading.

Using the `Accept` and `Content-Type` headers together to describe what can be understood by the client, and what was actually sent, is called content negotiation. Using the headers to negotiate the usable formats means that meta-information is not tangled up with actual data as it would be when sending both kinds of parameters with the body or URL of the request. Including the headers is generally a better approach.

We can negotiate more than just content, too. The earlier example contained these lines:

```
Accept-Encoding: gzip, deflate, sdch
Accept-Language: en-GB,en-US;q=0.8,en;q=0.6
Accept-Charset: ISO-8859-1,utf-8;q=0.7,*;q=0.3
```

These headers show other kinds of negotiation, such as declaring what encoding the client supports, which languages are preferred, and which character sets can be used. This enables decisions to be made about how to format the response in various ways, and how to determine which formats are appropriate for the consuming device.

Parsing an Accept Header

Let's start by looking at how to parse an `Accept` header correctly. All `Accept` headers have a comma-separated list of values, and some include a q value that indicates their level of preference. If the q value isn't included for an entry, it can be assumed that q=1 for that entry. Using the `Accept` header from my browser again, I can parse it by taking all the segments, working out their preferences, and then sorting them appropriately. Here's an example function that returns an array of supported formats in order of preference:

```php
<?php

function parseAcceptHeader() {
    $hdr = $_SERVER['HTTP_ACCEPT'];
    $accept = array();
    foreach (preg_split('/\s*,\s*/', $hdr) as $i => $term) {
        $o = new \stdclass;
        $o->pos = $i;
        if (preg_match(",^(\S+)\s*;\s*(?:q|level)=([0-9\.]+),i", $term, $M)) {
            $o->type = $M[1];
            $o->q = (double)$M[2];
        } else {
            $o->type = $term;
            $o->q = 1;
```

```
        }
        $accept[] = $o;
    }
    usort($accept, function ($a, $b) {
        /* first tier: highest q factor wins */
        $diff = $b->q - $a->q;
        if ($diff > 0) {
            $diff = 1;
        } else if ($diff < 0) {
            $diff = -1;
        } else {
            /* tie-breaker: first listed item wins */
            $diff = $a->pos - $b->pos;
        }
        return $diff;
    });
    $accept_data = array();
    foreach ($accept as $a) {
        $accept_data[$a->type] = $a->type;
    }
    return $accept_data;
}
```

 The headers sent by your browser may differ slightly and result in different output when you try the previous code snippet.

When using the Accept header sent by my browser, I see the following output:

```
Array
(
    [text/html] => text/html
    [application/xhtml+xml] => application/xhtml+xml
    [image/webp] => image/webp
    [application/xml] => application/xml
    [*/*] => */*
)
```

We can use this information to work out which format it would be best to send the data back in. For example, here's a simple script that calls the parseAcceptHeader() function, then works through the formats to determine which it can support, and sends that information:

```
<?php

require "accept.php";

$data = ["greeting" => "hello", "name" => "Lorna"];
```

```
$accepted_formats = parseAcceptHeader();
$supported_formats = ["application/json", "text/html"];
foreach($accepted_formats as $format) {
    if(in_array($format, $supported_formats)) {
        // yay, use this format
        break;
    }
}

switch($format) {
    case "application/json":
        header("Content-Type: application/json");
        $output = json_encode($data);
        break;
    case "text/html":
    default:
        $output = "<p>" . implode(', ', $data) . "</p>";
        break;
}

echo $output;
```

There are many, many ways to parse the Accept header (and the same techniques apply to the Accept-Language, Accept-Encoding, and Accept-Charset headers), but it is vital to do so correctly. The importance of Accept header parsing can be seen in Chris Shiflett's blog post, The Accept Header (*http://bit.ly/shiflett-accept-header*); the parseAcceptHeader() example shown previously came mostly from the comments on this post. You might use this approach, an existing library such as the PHP mimeparse port (*https://github.com/ramsey/mimeparse*), a solution you build yourself, or one offered by your framework. Whichever you choose, make sure that it parses these headers correctly, rather than using a string match or something similar.

Demonstrating Accept Headers with cURL

Using cURL from the command line, here are some examples of how to call exactly the same URL by setting different Accept headers and seeing different responses:

```
curl http://localhost/book/hello.php
hello, Lorna

curl -H "Accept: application/json" http://localhost/book/hello.php
{"greeting":"hello","name":"Lorna"}

curl -H "Accept: text/html;q=0.5,application/json"
http://localhost/book/hello.php
{"greeting":"hello","name":"Lorna"}
```

To make these requests from PHP rather than from cURL, it is possible to simply set the desired headers as the request is made. Here's an example that uses PHP's cURL extension to make the same request as the previous example:

```php
<?php

$url = "http://localhost/book/hello.php";

$ch = curl_init($url);
curl_setopt($ch, CURLOPT_HEADER, array(
    "Accept: text/html;q=0.5,application/json",
));
curl_setopt($ch, CURLOPT_RETURNTRANSFER, true);
$response = curl_exec($ch);
echo $response;
curl_close($ch);
```

The number of headers you need to support in your application will vary. It is common and recommended to offer various content types such as JSON, XML, or even plain text. The selection of supported encodings, languages, and character sets will depend entirely on your application and users' needs. If you do introduce support for variable content types, however, this is the best way to do it.

Securing Requests with the Authorization Header

Headers can provide information that allows an application to identify users. Again, keeping this type of information separate from the application data makes things simpler and, often, more secure. The key thing to remember when working on user security for APIs is that everything you already know about how to secure a website *applies to web services*. A common header that has been seen earlier in this book is the `Authorization` header. This can be used with a variety of different techniques for authenticating users, all of which will be familiar to web developers.

Rather than the `Authorization` header, some applications may have alternative approaches including using cookies and sessions to record a user's information after he has supplied credentials to a login endpoint, for example. Others will implement solutions of their own making, and many of these will use a simple *API key* approach. In this approach, the user acquires a key, often via a web interface or other means, that she can use when accessing the API. A major advantage of this approach is that the keys can be deleted by either party, or can expire, removing the likelihood that they can be used with malicious intent. This is nicer than passing actual user credentials, as the details used can be changed. Sometimes API keys will be passed simply as a query parameter, but the `Authorization` header would also be an appropriate place for such information.

HTTP Basic Authentication

The simplest approach to authorization is HTTP Basic authentication (for more details, see the RFC (*http://bit.ly/rfc1945-11*)), which requires the user to supply a username and password to identify himself. Since this approach is so widespread, it is well supported in most platforms, both client and server. Do beware, though, that these credentials can easily be inspected and reused maliciously, so this approach is appropriate only on trusted networks or over SSL.

When the user tries to access a protected resource using basic authentication, he will receive a 401 status code in response, which includes a WWW-Authenticate header with the value Basic followed by a *realm* for which to authenticate. As users, we see an unstyled pop up for username and password in our browser; this is basic authentication. When we supply the credentials, the client will combine them in the format username:password and Base64 encode the result before including it in the Authorization header of the request it makes.

The mechanism of the basic authentication is this:

1. Arrange the username and password into the format username:password.
2. Base64 encode the result.
3. Send it in the header, like this: Authorization: Basic *base64-encoded string*.
4. Since tokens are sent in plain text, HTTPS should be used throughout.

We can either follow the steps here and manually create the correct header to send, or we can use the built-in features of our toolchain. Here's PHP's cURL extension making a request to a page protected by basic authentication:

```php
<?php

$url = "http://localhost/book/basic-auth.php";

$ch = curl_init($url);
curl_setopt($ch, CURLOPT_HTTPAUTH, CURLAUTH_BASIC ) ;
curl_setopt($ch, CURLOPT_USERPWD, "user:pass");
curl_setopt($ch, CURLOPT_RETURNTRANSFER, true);
$response = curl_exec($ch);
echo $response;
curl_close($ch);
```

In PHP, these details can be found on the $_SERVER superglobal. When basic authentication is in use, the username and password supplied by the user can be found in $_SERVER["PHP_AUTH_USER"] and $_SERVER["PHP_AUTH_PW"], respectively. When a request is made without credentials, or with invalid credentials, a 401 Unauthorized status code can be sent to tell the client why the server is not sending him the content requested.

HTTP Digest Authentication

Similar to basic authentication, but rather more secure, is HTTP Digest authentication (the Wikipedia page (*https://en.wikipedia.org/wiki/Digest_access_authentication*) includes a great explanation with examples). This process combines the username and password with the realm, a client nonce (a nonce is a cryptographic term meaning "number used once"), a server nonce, and other information, and hashes them before sending. It may sound complicated to implement, but this standard is well understood and widely implemented by both clients and servers.

Very little changes when working with digest authentication when compared to the example of basic authentication just shown; the main things to look out for are:

- The `CURLOPT_HTTPAUTH` option should be set to `CURLAUTH_DIGEST`.
- On the receiving end, you can find the user data in `$_SERVER[`*`PHP_AUTH_DIGEST`*`]`, which will need decoding according to the type of digest authentication you are using.

Digest authentication is preferred over basic authentication unless the connection is over SSL. If you want to work with digest auth then there's a good resource on Sitepoint (*http://bit.ly/sitepoint-digest*).

OAuth

An even better solution has emerged in the last few years: OAuth (*http://oauth.net*) (version 2 is much better than version 1). OAuth arises as a solution to a very specific and common problem: how do we allow a third party (such as an external application on a mobile device) to have secure access to a user's data? This is solved by establishing a three-way relationship, so that requests coming to the providing API from the third-party consumer have access to the user's data, but do not impersonate that user. For every combination of application and user, the external application will send the user to the providing API to confirm that she wants access to be granted. Once the relationship is established, the user can, at any time, visit the providing API (with which she originally had the relationship of trust) to revoke that access. Newer versions of OAuth are simple to implement but, again, should *always* be used over SSL.

In OAuth terminology, we name the client the "consumer" and the server the "provider." The consumer could be a app on your smartphone for example, and the provider would then be the system where you already have an account such as GitHub. Features such as "Sign in with GitHub" use this approach.

The basic process looks something like this:

1. The user chooses to sign in with GitHub, or link their GitHub account to a third-party client.

2. The client forwards the user to the provider's page to sign in and give permission for this client to access the user's data.

3. The user does sign in and confirm, and arrives back in the app.

4. The client can then get an *access token* from the provider.

Once we have the access token, we send this in the `Authorization` header for every request, something like:

```
Authorization: Bearer 852990de317
```

This approach is elegant in two ways:

- The identity information is not sent as part of the body of the request. By sending this information in the header, we separate the two concerns.

- By using an access token rather than the user's actual credentials, we give the ability for that access token to expire or be revoked in the future. This allows users to safely grant access to even unknown applications and know that they can always remove that access in the future, even if that application doesn't offer the option to remove creds (or if the user doesn't trust it to), without needing to change the user's credentials and therefore break *all* of the integrations that use this account.

This solution is very widely used in APIs and is recommended if you need to authenticate users in your own applications.

Hopefully this serves to cover the overall concept of OAuth and how to use an access token in your own application. For a more complete explanation, the book *Getting Started with OAuth 2.0* (O'Reilly) is an excellent reference.

Caching Headers

Just like for other web requests, getting caching right can help enormously when an API server needs to handle a lot of traffic. Requests that perform actions cannot be cached, as they must be processed by the server each time, but `GET` requests certainly can be, in the right situation. Caching can either be done by the server, which makes a decision about whether to serve a previous version of a resource, or by clients storing the result of previous requests and allowing us to compare versions.

Giving version information along with a resource is a key ingredient in client-side caching, and also links with the nonatomic update procedures in REST as we mention in "Update a Resource with PUT" on page 87. When returning a resource, either an `ETag` (usually a hash of the representation itself) or a `Last-Modified` (the date this record last changed) is included with the response. Clients that understand these systems can then store these responses locally, and when making the same request again at a later point, they can tell us which version of a resource they already have. This is very similar to the way that web browsers cache assets such as stylesheets and images.

When a resource is served with an ETag header, this header will contain some textual representation of the resource, perhaps a hash of the resource or a combination of file size and timestamp. When requesting the resource at a later date, the client can send an If-None-Match header with the value of the ETag in it. If the current version of the resource has a nonmatching ETag, then the new resource will be returned with its ETag header. However if the ETag values do match, the server can simply respond with a 304 "Not Modified" status code and an empty body, indicating to the client that it can use the version it already has without transferring the new version. This can help reduce server load and network bandwidth.

In exactly the same way, a resource that is sent with a Last-Modified header can be stored with that header information by the client. A subsequent request would then have an If-Modified-Since header, with the current Last-Modified value in it. The server compares the timestamp it receives with the last update to the resource, and again either serves the resource with new metadata, or with the much smaller 304 response.

Custom Headers

As with almost every aspect of HTTP, the headers that can be used aren't set in stone. It is possible to invent new headers if there's more information to convey for which there isn't a header. Headers that aren't "official" can always be used (sometimes they are prefixed with X- but they don't have to be), so you can make use of this in your own applications if you wish.

A good example, often seen on the Web, is when a tool such as Varnish (*https://www.varnish-cache.org/*) has been involved in serving a response, and it adds its own headers. I have Varnish installed in front of my own site, and when I request it, I see:

```
HTTP/1.1 200 OK
Server: Apache/2.4.7 (Ubuntu)
X-Powered-By: PHP/5.5.9-1ubuntu4.6
X-Pingback: http://www.lornajane.net/xmlrpc.php
Content-Type: text/html; charset=UTF-8
Date: Sat, 11 Jul 2015 08:57:32 GMT
X-Varnish: 600227065 600227033
Age: 43
Via: 1.1 varnish
Connection: keep-alive
```

That additional X-Varnish header shows me that Varnish served the request. It isn't an official header, but these X-* headers are used to denote all kinds of things in APIs and on the Web. A great example comes from GitHub (*http://developer.github.com*).

Here's what happens when I make a request to fetch a list of the repositories associated with my user account (*https://api.github.com/users/lornajane/repos*):

```
HTTP/1.1 200 OK
Server: GitHub.com
Date: Sat, 11 Jul 2015 08:59:01 GMT
Content-Type: application/json; charset=utf-8
Content-Length: 157631
Status: 200 OK
X-RateLimit-Limit: 60
X-RateLimit-Remaining: 59
ETag: "8976d7fc7aa861a8581108e59ae76506"
X-GitHub-Media-Type: github.v3
X-GitHub-Request-Id: 5EC19EE1:61C0:10B4CDB:55A0DAD5
X-Content-Type-Options: nosniff
X-Served-By: 13d09b732ebe76f892093130dc088652
```

There are a few custom headers in this example but the `X-RateLimit-*` headers are particularly worth noting; they check whether too many requests are being made. Using custom headers like these, any additional data can be transferred between client and server that isn't part of the body data, which means all parties can stay "on the same page" with the data exchange.

Headers are particularly important when working with APIs as there is often separation between the data and the metadata. Not all APIs are designed that way, but look out for some examples in particular in Chapter 8.

CHAPTER 4

Cookies

The HTTP protocol is *stateless*. This means that every request made must include all the information needed in order for the web server to serve the correct responses (at least, in theory!). In practice, that isn't how we experience the Web as users. As we browse around a shopping site, the website "remembers" which products we already viewed and which we placed in our basket—we experience our journeys on the Web as connected experiences.

So how does this work? Additional information is being saved and sent with our web requests through the use of *cookies*. Cookies are just key/value pairs: simple variables that can be stored on the client and sent back to us with future requests. A user's choice of theme or accessibility settings could be stored, or a cookie could be dropped to record something as simple as whether the user has visited the site before, or dismissed a particular alert message that was shown.

In this chapter we'll look at how cookies work and how they fit into our existing knowledge of HTTP, then discuss how cookies are used in API design (spoiler alert: they're not).

Cookie Mechanics

This isn't the moment where I tell you how to bake cookies, although the instructions do read a little bit like a recipe. What happens when we work with cookies goes something like this (see Figure 4-1):

1. A request arrives from the client, without cookies.

2. Send the response, including cookie(s).

3. The next request arrives. Since cookies were already sent, they will be sent back to us in these later requests.

4. Send the next response, also with cookies (either changed or unchanged).

5. Steps 3–4 are repeated indefinitely.

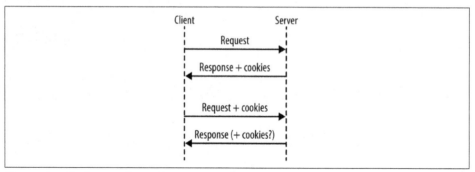

Figure 4-1. Cookies exchanged in a series of requests

The main thing to remember is that, for a first visit from a new client (or someone who clears their cookies), there will be no cookies, so it is not possible to rely on them being present. This is easy to miss in testing unless you consciously make the effort to also test the case in which a user arrives without cookies; by default, your browser will keep sending the cookies.

Another thing to note is that cookies are only sent back with subsequent requests *by convention*; not all clients will do this automatically. Once a cookie is received by a client, even if it isn't sent again in any later responses, most clients will send that cookie with each and every subsequent request. The most important thing to remember about cookies is that you *cannot trust* the data. When a cookie is sent to a client, it will be stored in plain text on that computer or device. Users can edit cookies as they please, or add and remove cookies, very easily. This makes incoming cookie data about as trustworthy as data that arrives on the URL with a GET request.

To put that a little more plainly: *do not trust cookie data.*

How do users edit their data? Well, there are a couple of options. First, let's look at using cookies with cURL. We can capture cookies into a "cookie jar" by using the -c switch. Take a look at what a well-known site like amazon.com sets for a new visitor:

```
curl -c cookies.txt http://www.amazon.com/
```

The cookie jar file that was saved will look something like this:

```
# Netscape HTTP Cookie File
# http://curl.haxx.se/rfc/cookie_spec.html
# This file was generated by libcurl! Edit at your own risk.

.amazon.com TRUE  /  FALSE  1355305311  skin             noskin
.amazon.com TRUE  /  FALSE  2082787201  session-id-time  2082787201l
.amazon.com TRUE  /  FALSE  2082787201  session-id       000-0000000-0000000
```

The format here contains the following elements:

- Domain the cookie is valid for
- Whether it is valid for all machines on this domain (usually TRUE)
- Path within the domain that this cookie is valid for
- Whether this cookie is only to be sent over a secure connection
- When this cookie will expire
- Name of the cookie
- Value of the cookie

Note the phrase "Edit at your own risk," which translates to developers as "Edit, and interesting things may happen." Whether working with a browser or cURL, it is possible to change these values wherever the cookies are stored, and they will be sent back to the server with a later request. With cURL, change the -c switch to a -b switch to send the cookies back with a request (use them both together to also capture incoming ones back into the file).

```
curl -b cookies.txt http://www.amazon.com/
```

In the browser, your options will vary depending on which browser you use, but all of the modern browsers have developer tools either built in or available via a plug-in that enables you to see and to change the cookies that are being sent, as was mentioned in "Browser Tools" on page 10. I use Chrome so I use the Edit This Cookie (*http://bit.ly/edit-this-cookie*) plug-in. Most browsers actually use an SQLite (*https://sqlite.org/*) database rather than a plain text file to store their cookies; however you can still edit this using standard SQLite tools.

Reading and Writing Cookies

Cookies are key/value pairs, as I've mentioned, that are sent to the browser along with some other information, such as which paths the cookie is valid for and when it expires. Since PHP is designed to solve "the Web problem," it has some great features for working with cookies. To set a cookie, use a function helpfully called set cookie():

```
<?php

setcookie("visited", true);
```

We can use this approach to show a welcome message to a visitor when he first comes to the site—because without any previous cookies, he won't have the "visited" cookie set. Once he has received one response from this server, his "visited" cookie will be seen on future requests. In PHP, cookies that arrived with a request can be found in the $_COOKIE superglobal variable. It is an array containing the keys and values of the cookies that were sent with the request. Following the preceding example we could read the cookie and the code would look something like this:

```php
<?php

var_dump($_COOKIE);

// 1st request: array(0) { }

// later requests: array(1) { ["visited"]=> string(1) "1" }
```

When working with APIs, the same facilities are available to us. When PHP is a server, the techniques of using setcookie and checking for values in $_COOKIE are all that are needed, exactly like when we are working with a standard web application. When consuming external services in PHP, it is possible to send cookie headers with our requests in the usual way.

Making Requests with Cookies

There's some nice support for sending cookies in PHP's cURL extension, which has a specific flag for setting cookies rather than just adding headers. With PHP's cURL extension, it is possible to do something like this:

```php
<?php

$url = "http://requestb.in/example";

$ch = curl_init($url);

curl_setopt($ch, CURLOPT_COOKIE, "visited=true");
curl_setopt($ch, CURLOPT_RETURNTRANSFER, true);
$result = curl_exec($ch);
curl_close($ch);
```

A selection of other options can be set using cookies, as seen when we discussed capturing them into the cookie jar in the code examples in "Cookie Mechanics" on page 41. The expiry date is probably the most-used setting. The expiry information is used to let the client know how long this cookie is valid for. After this time, the cookie will expire and not be sent with any later requests. This relies on the client and server clocks being vaguely in sync, which is often not the case. Having exactly matching clocks is rare, and in some cases clients can have their clocks set incorrectly by a number of years, so beware.

The expiry can be set in the past to *delete* a cookie that is no longer needed. If an expiry has not been set for a cookie, it becomes a "session cookie," which means that it is valid until the user closes the browser. This is why you should always close your browser on any machine or device that is used by others, even after logging out of your accounts.

Don't confuse the "session cookie" with the cookies PHP uses to track user sessions within a web application.

Cookies and APIs

It's very unusual to see a cookie used in APIs, and the reason for this is fundamental to APIs: they are *stateless*, as was already mentioned. Stateless means that they don't rely on information that is not part of this request; we don't follow on from information that went before or rely on a particular setting being in a particular state.

A stateless API cannot, by definition, use sessions either. These rely on information already having been exchanged and stored for a particular journey. Many PHP installations turn on sessions by default but this isn't appropriate for an API.

Having a stateless API also enables it to be "idempotent." Idempotency is the idea that you can repeat a request and achieve the same outcome each time.

One of the big side benefits of writing stateless services is that they scale horizontally really well. If you need more capacity on your API, you can deploy it to more servers, which all sit alongside one another with a load balancer in front to share the traffic between them. Since each incoming request contains all the information needed to process it, it doesn't matter which server it gets routed to and scaling up becomes easily achievable.

Designing a service this way does mean that we need to find alternative ways to implement some of the patterns we use sessions for in our other PHP applications. This could be:

- Using an access token or credentials to identify a user and looking up their details on every request rather than storing those in a session.
- The client needs to send information such as filtering and ordering preferences along with each request rather than expecting the information to already exist.

By making each request self-sufficient, we can scale up our services very flexibly since we don't rely on other resources.

CHAPTER 5

JSON

JSON stands for JavaScript Object Notation, but don't be fooled by the name. Although it sounds as if it's a JavaScript-specific format, it is supported by most programming languages today. It's a very simple, lightweight format, which can represent nested, structured data.

For example, consider a data set that looked like this:

- message
  — en: "hello friend"
  — es: "hola amigo"

In JSON, that data would look like this:

```
{"message":{"en":"hello friend","es":"hola amigo"}}
```

If a piece of data is represented by a scalar value, then it is presented plainly. If it is structured (as shown in the previous example), such as an associative array or an object with properties in PHP, a curly brace is used to indicate a new level of depth in the data structure. The keys and values are separated by colons, and each record at a given level is separated with a comma.

It is also possible to show a list of items quite elegantly using JSON. Take this imaginary shopping list:

- eggs
- bread
- milk
- bananas

- bacon

- cheese

A JSON representation of this would simply be:

```
["eggs","bread","milk","bananas","bacon","cheese"]
```

As you can see here, many of the keys in the previous example are optional, and multiple values are enclosed with the simple square brackets. If this list was in fact the value of a property, then both kinds of brackets would be seen:

```
{"list":["eggs","bread","milk","bananas","bacon","cheese"]}
```

This example shows that our data contained a key/value pair, with the key "list."

When to Choose JSON

JSON gives a very clear indication of the original data structure and conveys the values within, but doesn't give us any specific information about the exact data types that were originally in use. Often, this isn't important; HTTP is entirely string-based anyway so it is usual to deal with this type of data in web-based applications.

JSON's strongest point is that it is a simple data format. It doesn't take much storage space in comparison to XML and isn't too large to transfer "over the wire" or, in the case of mobile applications, over a potentially slow and patchy data connection! Since it is quite small and simple, it is inexpensive in processor terms to decode the JSON format, which makes it ideal for less powerful devices such as phones.

Use JSON when information about the exact data format isn't critical, and the effort needed to decode it must stay light. It's great for casual web or mobile applications—and of course it's absolutely ideal if you are supplying data to a JavaScript consumer, since it handles this data format natively and quickly.

Content negotiation over HTTP using headers has already been covered earlier in the book (see Chapter 3); this is how it is ascertained that the client would like a JSON response format. As an example, here are the headers for a request/response pair in which the consumer is requesting JSON and the API provides exactly that:

```
> GET /header.php HTTP/1.1
> Accept: application/json, text/html;=0.5

< HTTP/1.1 200 OK
< Content-Type: application/json

{"message":"hello there"}
```

You can see that the final entry in the example is the body of the response. The format of this is the same JSON that was covered earlier in this chapter. Setting the headers correctly is absolutely key, since without the correct Content-Type header, any application receiving this request will not know how to decode it. If it requested JSON, it might *hope* that's what was returned, but the Content-Type should always match. If it isn't specified, many web servers will default to sending a Content-Type of "text/html," which is not only inaccurate, but also dangerous because a browser will try to display the content as HTML and allow embedded JavaScript—so do take care to set those headers correctly.

Handling JSON with PHP

This is very simple, which is another reason to choose JSON as a preferred output format! In PHP, you can use json_encode() to turn either an array or an object into valid JSON.

For example, the previous example showed some JSON that looked like this:

```
{"message":"hello you"}
```

To generate that from PHP (which is exactly how I generated the previous examples), I simply used this line:

```
echo json_encode(array("message" => "hello you"));
```

This shows a very simple array wrapped in json_encode() and using echo to output it so I can see it when I request the page.

To handle incoming JSON data and turn it into a structure you can use, simply use json_decode(), passing the string containing the JSON as the first argument. Sticking with our existing simple example, the code could look something like this:

```
$data = json_decode('{"message":"hello you"}');
var_dump($data);
```

This example includes var_dump() to show *exactly* what actually happens when the json_decode() function is used: by default, an object is returned. Here's the output of that script:

```
object(stdClass)#1 (1) {
  ["message"]=>
  string(9) "hello you"
}
```

Because there is no data-type information, JSON cannot tell whether this was an array with keys and values, or an object with properties, before it was turned into JSON; there is no difference between the two. We would get identical output from a script that looked like this instead:

```
$obj = new stdClass();
$obj->message = "hello you";
echo json_encode($obj) . "\n";
```

Similarly, the same output would be shown if an object of any other class were used; the object-type information just isn't included in JSON so it can't be retrieved at the other end. When calling the json_decode(), it is possible to convert the data to an associative array rather than an object—by passing true as the optional second argument:

```
$data = json_decode('{"message":"hello you"}', true);
var_dump($data);
```

This time around, our output is subtly different:

```
array(1) {
  ["message"]=>
  string(9) "hello you"
}
```

Whether you choose to work with objects or arrays is up to you, and really depends on the application and also the language. Since there's no object-type information stored in JSON, the object produced by json_decode() is always StdClass and personally I find it easier to take an array and possibly hydrate a specific object type with that data.

The JSONSerializable Interface

PHP also offers a way of describing how an existing object will behave when passed json_encode(), which is a useful technique if you're outputting data that exists as an object in your application before it is output. It uses an interface called JSON Serializable; your object should implement this interface and include the jsonSeri alize() method. This method will be called when the object is converted to JSON.

Here's a simple example, starting with a very basic class that just adds the interface and defines what to do, then shows it in action:

```php
<?php

class gardenObject implements JsonSerializable
{
  public function jsonSerialize() {
    unset($this->herbs);
    return $this;
  }
}

$garden = new gardenObject();
$garden->flowers = array("clematis", "geranium", "hydrangea");
$garden->herbs = array("mint", "sage", "chives", "rosemary");
$garden->fruit = array("apple", "rhubarb");

echo json_encode($garden);
```

```
// {"flowers":["clematis","geranium","hydrangea"],"fruit":["apple","rhubarb"]}
```

This can be a very useful shortcut to quickly convert an object even if it needs a little customization before output.

Consuming JSON APIs

As an example of working with an API that uses JSON, let's take a look at a little piece of the GitHub API and use JSON for our examples. The examples here work with *gists* (*http://gist.github.com*), which are similar to "pastebins"—places where you can put code or other text to share with others.

Our example is very simple; we make a POST request and include some JSON in the body of the request. A POST request usually creates data, as you'll see in Chapter 8, and in this case we're creating a new gist:

```php
<?php

// grab the access token from an external file to avoid oversharing
require("github-creds.php");

$data = json_encode([
    'description' => 'Gist created by API',
    'public' => 'true',
    'files' => [
        'text.txt' => [ 'content' => 'Some riveting text' ]
    ]
]);

$url = "https://api.github.com/gists";
$ch = curl_init($url);

curl_setopt($ch, CURLOPT_POST, 1);
curl_setopt($ch, CURLOPT_POSTFIELDS, $data);
curl_setopt($ch, CURLOPT_HTTPHEADER,
    ['Content-Type: application/javascript',
   'Authorization: token ' . $access_token,
   'User-Agent: php-curl']
);
curl_setopt($ch, CURLOPT_RETURNTRANSFER, true);
$result = curl_exec($ch);
curl_close($ch);

$gist = json_decode($result, true);
if($gist) {
    echo "Your gist is at " . $gist['html_url'];
}
```

There are a few things going on here that bear closer examination: sending JSON in requests, working with an Authorization header, and using credentials to gain access. You will notice that a variable $access_token is referenced, which isn't set in the code. This is set in the *github-creds.php* file and kept separate to stop access keys from being leaked in this text. In a real development project, I'd still keep this separate, but for a different reason—using a separate file means I can exclude it from source control and avoid publicizing my access keys to the world! Of course it does happen, and if it does, you can always revoke your token and generate a new one. If you ever suspect that a token has been leaked, then do destroy it and generate another (something to bear in mind if your tokens are visible when demonstrating APIs).

A POST request is used to create a new gist (GitHub has a RESTful API) and send JSON-formatted data along with it. In fact, this is a PHP array (because those are easy to understand and work with), which is then converted to JSON using json_encode(). The resulting output is given as the value for CURLOPT_POSTFIELDS and PHP sends it as the body of the request.

This example also sets some headers using the CURLOPT_HTTPHEADER option. The first one is Content-Type, which we have already seen in many examples, and the second one is Authorization. The Authorization header here includes the "token" and the access token within it, because the GitHub API uses OAuth2 for authorization. We discussed OAuth in Chapter 3. The GitHub API also requires that a User-Agent header be sent so you will need to include this too if your PHP isn't already configured to send it by default.

If all goes well with the previous request, a 201 status code will arrive with the response and the new gist will be created. The gist will also be visible on the Web (*https://gist.github.com/*). Alternatively, the gist can be requested over the API: one of the things included in the response when requesting the new gist is a link to it, so we can extend the example to also fetch the gist. Since this is a public gist, no authorization is needed and it is possible to just grab the data using file_get_contents(), then json_decode() it. You could add the following code to the previous example to do exactly this:

```
if($gist) {
    echo file_get_contents($gist['url']);
}
```

You can easily try this yourself, or for an even simpler way to interact with the GitHub API, simply request all your own gists using *https://api.github.com/users/user name/gists* and replacing *username* with your own GitHub username. Many APIs use JSON in a similar way to exchange information with consumers, and you've now seen how to do that with PHP.

In addition to working purely with PHP, when working with JSON APIs you may find yourself wanting to construct, inspect, and otherwise manipulate JSON data. There are some tools we will discuss later in Chapter 11, notably jq and the Python json module, that can help with this task.

CHAPTER 6

XML

XML is another very common data format used with APIs, and should feel familiar to us as developers. Anyone who has spent much time with the Web will understand the "pointy brackets" style of XML and will be able to read it. XML is a rather verbose format; the additional punctuation and scope for attributes, character data, and nested tags can make for a slightly bigger data size than other formats.

XML has many more features than JSON, and can represent a great many more things. You'll see more of this in Chapter 7, where complex data types and namespaces will come into play. XML doesn't have to be complicated; simple data can also be easily represented, just as it is with JSON. Consider our shopping list again:

- eggs
- bread
- milk
- bananas
- bacon
- cheese

The XML representation of this list would be:

```
<?xml version="1.0"?>
<list>
  <item>eggs</item>
  <item>bread</item>
  <item>milk</item>
  <item>bananas</item>
  <item>bacon</item>
  <item>cheese</item>
</list>
```

Working with XML in PHP isn't quite as easy as working with JSON was, because XML is more complicated. To produce the previous example, the code in Example 6-1 was used.

Example 6-1. Working with XML

```php
<?php

$list = array(
        "eggs",
        "bread",
        "milk",
        "bananas",
        "bacon",
        "cheese"
);

$xml = new SimpleXMLElement("<list />");
foreach($list as $item) {
    $xml->addChild("item", $item);
}

// for nice output
$dom = dom_import_simplexml($xml)->ownerDocument;
$dom->formatOutput = true;
echo $dom->saveXML();
```

The starting point is the array that will be our list. Next, a `SimpleXMLElement` object is instantiated with a root tag that forms the basis for the document. In XML, everything has to be in a tag, so an `<item>` tag has been introduced in order to contain each list item.

The final block only makes the output prettier, which isn't usually important because XML is for machines, not for humans. To get the XML to convert from a `SimpleXMLElement` object, call the `asXML()` method on that object, which returns a string. The string, however, is all on one line!

The previous example instead converted from `SimpleXMLElement` to `DOMElement`, and then grabbed the `DOMDocument` from that. Set the `formatOutput` to true, so when a call is made to `DOMDocument::saveXML()` (to ask it to return the XML as a string), the resulting output will be nicely formatted.

XML's abilities to represent attributes, children, and character data all provide a more powerful and descriptive way to represent data than, for example, JSON. These same features make XML a great way to represent very detailed information, including data-type information, so it's a great choice when those details really do matter. It can include information about the types of data and custom data types, and each element can have attributes to describe specific properties of an element. XML also supports namespaces that are sometimes used in complex data types (beware that namespaces are better supported by DOM in PHP than by SimpleXML).

The larger data format is less of a concern when working with powerful machines and fast network connections, so XML is a popular choice when exchanging data between computers or servers, rather than sending things to phones or web browsers. Do be aware, however, that bandwidth costs may well still apply and may be a significant cost factor when large amounts of data are being transferred.

APIs are all about integration between systems and sometimes the choice of data format will be dictated by whatever is on the other end of the relationship. XML is particularly popular among many enterprise technology platforms such as Java, Oracle, and .NET, so users of these technologies will often request XML as a preferred format. If you are working with products or people that would prefer XML or are more confident handling this format, then offer XML, even if only as one of multiple data format options in your API.

XML in PHP

There are many ways we can work with XML in PHP, and they're all useful in different situations. There are three main approaches to choose from and they all have their advantages and disadvantages:

1. *SimpleXML* is the most approachable, and my personal favorite. It is easy to use and understand, is well documented, and provides a simple interface (as the name suggests) for getting the job done. SimpleXML does have some limitations, but it is recommended for most applications.

2. *DOM* is handy when a project encounters some of the limitations in SimpleXML. It's more powerful and therefore more complicated to use, but there are a small number of operations that can't be done with SimpleXML. There are built-in functions to allow conversion between these two formats, so it's very common to use a combination of both in applications, as we saw earlier in Example 6-1.

3. *XMLReader, XMLWriter, and their sister XMLParser* are lower-level ways of dealing with XML. In general, these tools are complicated and unintuitive but they have a *major* advantage: they are streams-based and therefore don't load the entire XML document into memory at once. If very large data sets are involved, then this approach will be your friend.

Creating XML

There are a few libraries around but let's look at some examples of how to create a simple XML document. We'll be aiming to output sample output with a mixture of elements and attributes, as seen in Example 6-2.

Example 6-2. Sample XML document to use for our examples

```
<?xml version="1.0" ?>
<hotels>
        <hotel name="Queens Hotel">
                <rooms>17</rooms>
                <price>150</price>
        </hotel>
        <hotel name="Kings Hotel">
                <rooms>12</rooms>
                <price>150</price>
        </hotel>
        <hotel name="Grand Hotel">
                <rooms>27</rooms>
                <price>100</price>
        </hotel>
</hotels>
```

Usually we generate XML from stored data, but here are some examples with hardcoded values so you can see very clearly just the XML parts on their own. In a real
application, you'd use all the XML functionality I'm showing here, with loops to select
data from a database. First, look at Example 6-3 for an example of creating this in
SimpleXML.

Example 6-3. Create a sample XML document using SimpleXML in PHP

```php
<?php

$document = new SimpleXMLElement("<hotels />");

$kings = $document->addChild("hotel");
$kings->addAttribute("name", "Kings Hotel");
$kings->addChild("rooms", 12);
$kings->addChild("price", 150);

$queens = $document->addChild("hotel");
$queens->addAttribute("name", "Queens Hotel");
$queens->addChild("rooms", 17);
$queens->addChild("price", 150);

$grand = $document->addChild("hotel");
$grand->addAttribute("name", "Grand Hotel");
$grand->addChild("rooms", 27);
$grand->addChild("price", 100);
```

This is fairly straightforward and easy to follow. Example 6-4 uses the DOM extension instead, which is a bit longer.

Example 6-4. Create a sample XML document using PHP's DOM extension

```php
<?php

$document = new DOMDocument();
$hotels = $document->createElement('hotels');
$document->appendChild($hotels);

$kings = $document->createElement("hotel");
$name = $document->createAttribute('name');
$name->value = "Kings Hotel";
$kings->appendChild($name);
$rooms = $document->createElement("rooms", 12);
$kings->appendChild($rooms);
$price = $document->createElement("price", 150);
$kings->appendChild($price);

$hotels->appendChild($kings);

$queens = $document->createElement("hotel");
$name = $document->createAttribute('name');
$name->value = "Queens Hotel";
$queens->appendChild($name);
$rooms = $document->createElement("rooms", 17);
$queens->appendChild($rooms);
$price = $document->createElement("price", 150);
$queens->appendChild($price);

$hotels->appendChild($queens);

$grand = $document->createElement("hotel");
$name = $document->createAttribute('name');
$name->value = "Grand Hotel";
$grand->appendChild($name);
$rooms = $document->createElement("rooms", 27);
$grand->appendChild($rooms);
$price = $document->createElement("price", 100);
$grand->appendChild($price);

$hotels->appendChild($grand);
```

The DOM example is longer and for this trivial example it can seem quite clunky. It's worth including, though, since if you work with advanced XML services and especially if you need to work with namespaces and do complex manipulation of XML (for example, you can only change the order of nodes with DOM), then this extension will be an excellent approach.

Converting between SimpleXML and DOM extensions is very simple; I often do this in my own applications where most of the work can be done with SimpleXML, but perhaps just one more piece of advanced functionality is required from DOM. PHP offers the functions `dom_import_simplexml()` and `simplexml_import_dom()` so you can easily switch between the two rather than being locked into one or the other in a particular project.

Consuming XML APIs

We'll look at a specific example shortly (the Flickr kitten photos) but first let's take a look at how we can use PHP to get data from an XML document.

Parsing XML

We've seen how to create XML already. Let's use the same document and do the opposite: translate the XML into data we can use. SimpleXML is a really excellent way to parse XML and Example 6-5 has an example of how that could look.

Example 6-5. Parse our sample XML with SimpleXML

```php
<?php

$xml = new SimpleXMLElement(file_get_contents("sample.xml"));

echo("List of Hotels:\n");

foreach($xml->children() as $hotel) {
        echo $hotel['name'];
        echo " has " . $hotel->rooms . " rooms";
        echo " and costs " . $hotel->price. " EUR per night";
        echo "\n";
}
```

 When working with SimpleXML, be aware that properties such as rooms and price in the preceding example are actually of type Sim pleXMLElement. You will need to cast them to strings, either by echoing as done here, or by expressly casting the values so you can assign or return them.

If you need to parse a very large XML document (bigger than the memory PHP has available) then check out the XMLReader functionality in PHP. This works using streams, which means you don't need to load the entire document into memory to work on it. For all other cases, SimpleXML is a great idea and regular expressions are never recommended for parsing XML. Now that we've got our tools ready, let's move on to look at a real example.

Flickr's XML API

There are a wide variety of APIs using XML. This next example looks at the photo-sharing site Flickr (*http://flickr.com*). The Flickr API provides a wide variety of functionality for working with photos, and every language will have some classes available that you can use with it, but there's no reason not to interact with the API directly. Example 6-6 shows how to find a list of kitten pictures.

Example 6-6. Fetching data from Flickr's XMLRPC service

```php
<?php

require("api-key.php");
$animal = "kitten";
$data = file_get_contents('https://api.flickr.com/services/rest/?'
    . http_build_query(array(
        "method" => "flickr.photos.search",
        "api_key" => $api_key,
        "tags" => $animal,
        "format" => "xmlrpc",
        "per_page" => 6
    ))
);
```

This example requests all the newest photos tagged "kitten" from Flickr. It relies on another file called *api-key.php* that simply defines the $api_key variable; it's separate to make it easier to avoid accidentally sharing it or adding it to my git repository.

Flickr uses an API key passed as a URL parameter, which is a different approach than the Authorization header examples that have been demonstrated so far; each API will implement this in a different way. Although the header is a better practice, the developers of Flickr were trailblazers with implementing APIs for users, so there was no best practice when it was built. Since it's simply a GET request, this example uses file_get_contents() to fetch the carefully crafted URL. The resulting response looks something like this:

```
<?xml version="1.0" encoding="utf-8" ?>
<methodResponse>
        <params>
                <param>
                        <value>
                                <string>
&lt;photos page=&quot;1&quot; pages=&quot;81588&quot; perpage=&quot;6&quot;
total=&quot;489527&quot;&gt;
        &lt;photo id=&quot;19456951044&quot; owner=&quot;130395922@N06&quot;
secret=&quot;5986d9cdf8&quot; server=&quot;505&quot; farm=&quot;1&quot;
title=&quot;Lounging&quot; ispublic=&quot;1&quot; isfriend=&quot;0&quot;
        isfamily=&quot;0&quot; /&gt;
        &lt;photo id=&quot;19890527230&quot; owner=&quot;41867033@N00&quot;
secret=&quot;7863b99ca0&quot; server=&quot;276&quot; farm=&quot;1&quot;
title=&quot;Sholai, Kodaikanal, Cats&quot; ispublic=&quot;1&quot;
isfriend=&quot;0&quot;
        isfamily=&quot;0&quot; /&gt;
```

```
&lt;photo id=&quot;19455867524&quot; owner=&quot;41867033@N00&quot;
secret=&quot;400c7ba669&quot; server=&quot;428&quot; farm=&quot;1&quot;
title=&quot;Sholai, Kodaikanal, Cats&quot; ispublic=&quot;1&quot;
isfriend=&quot;0&quot; isfamily=&quot;0&quot; /&gt;
        &lt;photo id=&quot;20083899801&quot; owner=&quot;41867033@N00&quot;
secret=&quot;89e2242440&quot; server=&quot;328&quot; farm=&quot;1&quot;
title=&quot;Sholai, Kodaikanal, Cats&quot; ispublic=&quot;1&quot;
isfriend=&quot;0&quot; isfamily=&quot;0&quot; /&gt;
        &lt;photo id=&quot;20083891431&quot; owner=&quot;41867033@N00&quot;
secret=&quot;bf47f466ec&quot; server=&quot;429&quot; farm=&quot;1&quot;
title=&quot;Sholai, Kodaikanal, Cats&quot; ispublic=&quot;1&quot;
isfriend=&quot;0&quot; isfamily=&quot;0&quot; /&gt;
        &lt;photo id=&quot;19457506953&quot; owner=&quot;41867033@N00&quot;
secret=&quot;98b030686f&quot; server=&quot;477&quot; farm=&quot;1&quot;
title=&quot;Sholai, Kodaikanal, Cats&quot; ispublic=&quot;1&quot;
isfriend=&quot;0&quot; isfamily=&quot;0&quot; /&gt;
&lt;/photos&gt;
                                </string>
                        </value>
                </param>
        </params>
</methodResponse>
```

Because the data is sent as an escaped XML string, the XML is parsed in PHP, then the string is extracted and parsed as a separate step in order to obtain the real data. Flickr doesn't supply the actual URL of the image, but gives enough information in the response that the instructions (*http://bit.ly/flickr-source-urls*) can be followed to assemble the desired URL. SimpleXML is used in this example—first to parse the response, then to parse the data inside it. This library represents child elements as object properties (and each child is a `SimpleXMLElement`), while attributes are accessed using array notation.

Here's Example 6-6 again, processing the data and outputting it with titles and `<img>` tags:

```php
<?php

require("api-key.php");
$animal = "kitten";
$data = file_get_contents('http://api.flickr.com/services/rest/?'
    . http_build_query(array(
        "method" => "flickr.photos.search",
        "api_key" => $api_key,
        "tags" => $animal,
        "format" => "xmlrpc",
        "per_page" => 6
    ))
);

$simplexml = new SimpleXMLElement($data);
$data_array = $simplexml->params->param->value->children();
```

```
$photos = new SimpleXMLElement($data_array->string);

if($photos) {
    foreach($photos->photo as $photo) {
        echo $photo['title'] . "\n";
        echo '<img src="http://farm' . $photo['farm'] . '.staticflickr.com/'
            . $photo['server'] . '/' .$photo['id'] . '_' . $photo['secret']
            . '.jpg" /><br />' . "\n";
    }
}
```

The main body of the data contains a <photos> tag with multiple <photo> tags inside it—one for each photo. Each <photo> tag has some attributes inside it, so array notation is used to access these, retrieve the title, and build the image tag.

When working with APIs, you will see different data formats in use in a variety of settings. This chapter has shown how to create, work with, and parse XML. XML is more common on older and larger applications, but the data format will depend on the target market of the API, and many providers will offer multiple formats. Flickr, for example, offers data in both JSON and XML format, but also offers a serialized PHP format. PHP's serialized format is very easy to work with and is a great choice for two PHP applications exchanging data; if you were to integrate Flickr into your own PHP application, this would be good format to choose. When integrating with applications on other technology platforms, XML is a better-supported choice.

CHAPTER 7

RPC and SOAP Services

In this chapter we'll be looking at two closely related types of services: Remote Procedure Call (RPC) services, and SOAP. These two feel fairly similar, as they both involve calling functions and passing parameters, but their implementations are in stark contrast as RPC is a very loose way of describing a service, whereas SOAP is very tightly specified.

RPC

RPC services quite literally *call procedures* (i.e., functions) *remotely*. These types of API will typically have a single endpoint, so all requests are made to the same URL. Each request will include the name of the function to call, and may include some parameters to pass to it. Working with RPC services should feel familiar to us as developers because we know how to call functions—we simply do so over HTTP.

To start out, consider Example 6-6 when a call was made to Flickr. The URL we made for that example was:

```
http://api.flickr.com/services/rest/?method=flickr.photos.search&tags=
kitten&format=xmlrpc
```

Within the URL, the name of the function can be seen in the "method" parameter (`flickr.photos.search`), the particular tags to search for are found in `tags=`, and the `format` parameter asks for the response in XML-RPC format.

There is a distinct difference between using an RPC-style service, with function names and parameters included in the data supplied, and having a service that is true XML-RPC (*https://en.wikipedia.org/wiki/XML-RPC*), which is a very defined format. The option you choose depends entirely on the situation you and your application find yourselves in, but whichever it is, be sure to label it correctly.

Building an RPC service layer for an application can be achieved very simply by wrapping a class and exposing it over HTTP. Example 7-1 shows a very basic class that offers some toy functionality to use in the following examples.

Example 7-1. Library class example

```php
<?php

class Events
{
    protected $events = array(
        1 => array("name" => "Excellent PHP Event",
            "date" => 1454994000,
            "location" => "Amsterdam"
        ),
        2 => array("name" => "Marvellous PHP Conference",
            "date" => 1454112000,
            "location" => "Toronto"),
        3 => array("name" => "Fantastic Community Meetup",
            "date" => 1454894800,
            "location" => "Johannesburg"
        )
    );

    /**
     * Get all the events we know about
     *
     * @return array The collection of events
     */
    public function getEvents() {
        return $this->events;
    }

    /**
     * Fetch the detail for a single event
     *
     * @param int $event_id The identifier of the event
     *
     * @return array The event data
     */
    public function getEventById($event_id) {
        if(isset($this->events[$event_id])) {
            return $this->events[$event_id];
        } else {
            throw new Exception("Event not found");
        }
    }
}
```

To make this available via an RPC-style service, a simple wrapper can be written for it, which looks at the incoming parameters and calls the relevant function. You could use something along these lines:

```php
<?php

require "Events.php";

// look for a valid action
if(isset($_GET['method'])) {
    switch($_GET['method']) {
        case "eventList":
            $events = new Events();
            $data = $events->getEvents();
            break;
        case "event":
            $event_id = (int)$_GET['event_id'];
            $events = new Events();
            $data = $events->getEventById($event_id);
            break;
        default:
            http_response_code(400);
            $data = array("error" => "bad request");
            break;
    }
} else {
    http_response_code(400);
    $data = array("error" => "bad request");
}

// let's send the data back
header("Content-Type: application/json");
echo json_encode($data);
```

This example does a very simple switch-case on the incoming "action" parameter and passes in any variables as required (with validation, of course). We fetch the return data from the underlying library, then send the appropriate content negotiation headers and the data, formatted as JSON. If the request isn't understood, then a 400 status code is returned along with some error information.

The previous example shows a very simple RPC-style service using JSON, and illustrates how easy it is to wrap an existing class of functionality and expose it over HTTP. Sometimes it's appropriate to use HTTP *within* an application to allow different components to be scaled independently (for example, moving comments to a separate storage area to be accessed by the original application rather than HTTP). In those scenarios, this approach of wrapping existing, hardened code can be very useful indeed, and is quick to implement.

Exactly as the difference between XML over an RPC service and XML-RPC is important to remember, the same applies here. The example shows JSON being returned by an RPC service, but JSON-RPC (*https://en.wikipedia.org/wiki/JSON-RPC*) is something much more tightly specified (there's also XML-RPC). The *-RPC services can be a better choice when working with people or technologies that understand those and are happy implementing them. If the requirements are for something rather lighter and more approachable, then a simple custom format will work perfectly well. Standards are always good, especially for externally available systems, but don't feel that they are your only choice.

SOAP

SOAP was once an acronym for Simple Object Access Protocol; however, this has been dropped and now it is just "SOAP." SOAP is an RPC-style service that communicates over a very tightly specified format of XML. Since SOAP is well-specified when it follows WSDL conventions, little work is needed to implement it in an application, or to integrate against it; PHP has a really excellent set of SOAP libraries for both client and server.

You will see quite a few providers of SOAP implementations, and some open source tools such as SugarCRM and Magento also offer SOAP integration points. When looking at a new SOAP service, a tool called SoapUI (*http://www.soapui.org*) allows for browsing a service when a Web Service Description Language (WSDL) file is supplied. In fact, SoapUI is excellent and can do about a hundred other things, including complicated functional testing, but for now we will look at its SOAP functionality.

As an example, I took the WSDL file from RadioReference (*http://radioreference.com*) and added it into SoapUI, simply creating a new project, naming the project, and giving the URL to the WSDL file for this service. By default, this will create a request for each of the available methods, and generate an easy interface in which they can be executed. To run one, pick it from the list on the left, and then click the green Play button above the sample request. I used `getCountryList` as an example, as you can see in Figure 7-1.

The left half of the main pane shows the request that was sent, and the right half shows the response that was received. This gives a quick overview of how things look when using this API from our PHP code.

WSDL

This is a good moment to talk about the WSDL files that always seem to be mentioned whenever SOAP comes up. When it was first mentioned in this chapter, the acronym was defined as "Web Service Description Language," and this is a pretty good description of what is found in a WSDL file. It describes the location of a particular service, the data types that are used in it, and the methods, parameters, and return values that are available. The WSDL format is rather unfriendly XML, so it is best generated and parsed by machines rather than humans. If you do find yourself in the situation of needing to read one, it usually makes more sense to begin at the end of the document and then read upwards.

WSDL files are commonly used with SOAP, but they can be used with other types of web services. SOAP can also be used without a WSDL file, known in PHP as "non-WSDL mode." This chapter includes examples of SOAP with and without WSDLs, and an example of generating a WSDL file.

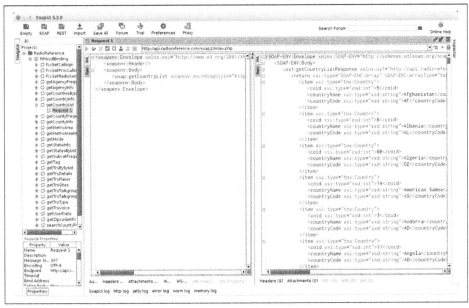

Figure 7-1. SoapUI showing a request to getCountryList

PHP SOAP Client

Returning to the countries list, we can acquire it from PHP quite easily using the SOAP extension. Take a look at this example, which does exactly that:

```php
<?php

$client = new SoapClient('http://api.radioreference.com/soap2/?wsdl&v=latest');

$countries = $client->getCountryList();
print_r($countries);
```

Simply using `print_r()` doesn't create a very pretty output, but it does illustrate what these two lines of PHP have produced. The beginning of the output looks like this:

```
Array
(
    [0] => stdClass Object
        (
            [coid] => 5
            [countryName] => Afghanistan
            [countryCode] => AF
        )

    [1] => stdClass Object
        (
            [coid] => 8
            [countryName] => Albania
            [countryCode] => AL
        )

    [2] => stdClass Object
        (
            [coid] => 60
            [countryName] => Algeria
            [countryCode] => DZ
        )

    [3] => stdClass Object
        (
            [coid] => 14
            [countryName] => American Samoa
            [countryCode] => AS
        )
```

Our two lines of PHP connected to a remote service and fetched us an array of objects containing the country information as requested. This shows the joy of SOAP, which is that very few lines of code are needed to exchange data between systems. The SoapClient class in PHP makes consuming data with a WSDL file trivial.

PHP SOAP Server

What about when we want to publish our own services? Well, PHP has a SoapServer that is almost as easy to use. Using the example library code from Example 7-1 to supply the underlying functionality, we can publish a SOAP service like this:

```php
<?php

require('Events.php');

$options = array("uri" => "http://localhost");

$server = new SoapServer(null, $options);
```

```
$server->setClass('Events');
$server->handle();
```

Since a WSDL is not used in the previous example, the Uniform Resource Identifier (URI) for the service must be provided. The example then creates the SoapServer and tells it which class holds the functionality it should expose. When the call to han dle() is added, everything "just works." The PHP to call the code looks much like the previous example, but without a WSDL file, it is necessary to tell the SoapClient where to find the service by setting the location parameter and passing the URI:

```php
<?php

$options = array("location" => "http://localhost:8080/soap-server.php",
    "uri" => "http://localhost");

try {
    $client = new SoapClient(null, $options);
    $events = $client->getEvents();
    print_r($events);
} catch (SoapFault $e) {
    var_dump($e);
}
```

Again, just doing a print_r() does show the results that are returned very clearly, but it isn't particularly pretty! The list of events shows like this:

```
Array
(
    [1] => Array
        (
            [name] => Excellent PHP Event
            [date] => 1454994000
            [location] => Amsterdam
        )

    [2] => Array
        (
            [name] => Marvellous PHP Conference
            [date] => 1454112000
            [location] => Toronto
        )

    [3] => Array
        (
            [name] => Fantastic Community Meetup
            [date] => 1454894800
            [location] => Johannesburg
        )

)
```

At this point, a working SOAP service exists, but not the WSDL file that is commonly used with it. The WSDL file holds the description of the service functionality, which means a file is created to describe our service, and should be re-created if any of the functions available change or if anything is added. Many technology stacks, such as Java and .NET, offer built-in functionality that makes it very easy to work with services that use WSDL files.

Generating a WSDL File from PHP

There are various solutions for generating a WSDL file from your library class code; some IDEs such as Eclipse have a button for it, and some frameworks also have this functionality. The examples here use a tool that will work regardless of the IDE or framework you use, because it's written in PHP and installed via Composer.

These examples are in their own directory so there's a single entry in the *composer.json* file:

```
{
    "require": {
        "php2wsdl/php2wsdl": "~0.3"
    }
}
```

Use Composer to install the dependencies (see http://getcomposer.org if you're not familiar with Composer) and then we have the tools that our WSDL-generating code relies on. To create the WSDL for the Events class from earlier, the code in Example 7-2 can be used.

Example 7-2. Generating WSDL code from an existing PHP class

```php
<?php

require "vendor/autoload.php";

// include the class we want to use
require "../Events.php";

$gen = new \PHP2WSDL\PHPClass2WSDL("Events", "http://localhost:8080/soap-
server2.php");
$gen->generateWSDL();

file_put_contents("wsdl", $gen->dump());
```

The code first includes the Composer autoloader, then the class that we're going to generate the WSDL from. Then we instantiate a new PHPClass2WSDL object and tell it firstly which class it is, and then pass a second parameter to explain what URL the WSDL will be available on. Once the WSDL has been generated, it simply writes it to a file that we could publish on our web server.

The outputted WSDL looks something like this:

```xml
<?xml version="1.0"?>
<definitions xmlns="http://schemas.xmlsoap.org/wsdl/" xmlns:tns="http://local
host:8080/wsdl" xmlns:soap="http://schemas.xmlsoap.org/wsdl/soap/"
xmlns:xsd="http://www.w3.org/2001/XMLSchema" xmlns:soap-enc="http://sche
mas.xmlsoap.org/soap/encoding/" xmlns:wsdl="http://schemas.xmlsoap.org/wsdl/"
name="Events" targetNamespace="http://localhost:8080/wsdl">
  <types>
    <xsd:schema targetNamespace="http://localhost:8080/wsdl">
      <xsd:import namespace="http://schemas.xmlsoap.org/soap/encoding/"/>
    </xsd:schema>
  </types>
  <portType name="EventsPort">
    <operation name="getEvents">
      <documentation>Get all the events we know about</documentation>
      <input message="tns:getEventsIn"/>
      <output message="tns:getEventsOut"/>
    </operation>
    <operation name="getEventById">
      <documentation>Fetch the detail for a single event</documentation>
      <input message="tns:getEventByIdIn"/>
      <output message="tns:getEventByIdOut"/>
    </operation>
  </portType>
  <binding name="EventsBinding" type="tns:EventsPort">
    <soap:binding style="rpc" transport="http://schemas.xmlsoap.org/soap/http"/>
    <operation name="getEvents">
      <soap:operation soapAction="http://localhost:8080/wsdl#getEvents"/>
      <input>
        <soap:body use="encoded" encodingStyle="http://schemas.xmlsoap.org/soap/
encoding/" namespace="http://localhost:8080/wsdl"/>
      </input>
      <output>
        <soap:body use="encoded" encodingStyle="http://schemas.xmlsoap.org/soap/
encoding/" namespace="http://localhost:8080/wsdl"/>
      </output>
    </operation>
    <operation name="getEventById">
      <soap:operation soapAction="http://localhost:8080/wsdl#getEventById"/>
      <input>
        <soap:body use="encoded" encodingStyle="http://schemas.xmlsoap.org/soap/
encoding/" namespace="http://localhost:8080/wsdl"/>
      </input>
      <output>
        <soap:body use="encoded" encodingStyle="http://schemas.xmlsoap.org/soap/
encoding/" namespace="http://localhost:8080/wsdl"/>
      </output>
    </operation>
  </binding>
  <service name="EventsService">
    <port name="EventsPort" binding="tns:EventsBinding">
      <soap:address location="http://localhost:8080/wsdl"/>
```

```
      </port>
    </service>
    <message name="getEventsIn"/>
    <message name="getEventsOut">
      <part name="return" type="soap-enc:Array"/>
    </message>
    <message name="getEventByIdIn">
      <part name="event_id" type="xsd:int"/>
    </message>
    <message name="getEventByIdOut">
      <part name="return" type="soap-enc:Array"/>
    </message>
  </definitions>
```

The WSDL as it stands isn't terribly descriptive, as it can't guess what data types could be used or whether the methods should have arguments or return values. This is because PHP is dynamically typed: data types are not declared when defining variables or passing them into functions, and data types of return values are not declared either. Some other languages do declare data types and WSDL files usually contain detailed type information.

As an aside, look out for WSDL files with data types that PHP doesn't support—if the client or server is not in PHP, there can be a mismatch of formats in some cases. This is the main reason why so many WSDL files have fairly loose types, with strings rather than anything more specific. In fact, I have also seen an entire web service with a WSDL file that described a single method and accepted a custom XML format within it, for exactly this reason—not fun!

In order to make WSDL files more accurate, phpDocumentor (*http://www.phpdoc.org*) comments can be added to our source code. Where the data types for parameters and return values are specified in documentation, the WSDL file will change to reflect the additional information. Code written to work with the type hinting and return values in PHP7 will also be able to produce clearer WSDLs when the tools update to support this.

PHP Client and Server with WSDL

Now there is a WSDL file to use with the Events example class, and the client and server code can be altered to take advantage of this. First, here's the server, with only the constructor needing to change:

```php
<?php

require('Events.php');

$server = new SoapServer("wsdl"); // wsdl file name
$server->setClass('Events');
$server->handle();
```

With the WSDL file in use, there's no need to give any other information. Just give the filename (this can be remote if appropriate) and all the location and other settings are picked up from there. The client can do exactly the same:

```php
<?php

try {
    $client = new SoapClient("http://localhost:8080/wsdl");
    $events = $client->getEvents();
    print_r($events);
} catch (SoapFault $e) {
    var_dump($e);
}
```

At this point, you're able to either build or consume RPC-style services in general, and XML-RPC, JSON-RPC, and SOAP in particular, with the use of handy tools such as SoapUI.

CHAPTER 8

REST

REST stands for REpresentational State Transfer, and in contrast to protocols such as SOAP or XML-RPC, it is more a philosophy or a set of principles than a protocol in its own right. REST is a set of ideas about how data can be transferred elegantly, and although it's not tied to HTTP, it is discussed here in the context of HTTP. REST takes great advantage of the features of HTTP, so the earlier chapters covering this and the more detailed topics of headers and verbs can all come together to support a good knowledge of REST.

In a RESTful service, four HTTP verbs are used to provide a basic set of CRUD (Create, Read, Update, Delete) functionality: POST, GET, PUT, and DELETE. It is also possible to see implementations of other verbs in RESTful services, such as PATCH to allow partial update of a record, but the basic four provide the platform of a RESTful service.

The operations are applied to *resources* in a system. The "Representational State Transfer" name is accurate; RESTful services deal in *transferring representations* of resources. A representation might be JSON or XML, or indeed anything else. So what is a resource? Well, everything is. Each individual data record in a system is a resource. At the first stage of API design, a starting point could be to consider each database row as an individual resource. Think of an imaginary blogging system as an example: resources might be posts, categories, and authors. Every resource has a URI, which is the unique identifier for the record.

A *collection* contains multiple resources (of the same type); usually this is a list of resources or the result of a search operation. A blog example might have a collection of posts, and another collection of posts limited to a particular category.

RESTful URLs

RESTful services are often thought of as "pretty URL" services, but there's more than prettiness to the structures used here. In Chapter 5, the GitHub API was used as an example of an API using JSON; it is also a nice example of a RESTful API belonging to a system that developers may already be familiar with. Take a look at some of the URLs in this API:

- *https://api.github.com/users/lornajane/*
- *https://api.github.com/users/lornajane/repos*
- *https://api.github.com/users/lornajane/gists*

These delightful, descriptive URLs allow users to guess what will be found when visiting them, and to easily navigate around a predictable and clearly designed system. They describe what data will be found there, and what to expect. A key characteristic of RESTful URLs is that they only contain information about the resource or collection data—*there are no verbs* in these URLs. The best of API designs will have URLs that are "hackable"—that is to say that they are predictable enough to successfully guess where to find things. This links closely to the idea of hypermedia, which we'll discuss shortly.

In order to alter how a collection is viewed (for example, to add filtering or sorting to it), it is common to add query parameters to the URL, like so:

- *http://api.joind.in/v2.1/events* for all events
- *http://api.joind.in/v2.1/events?filter=past* for events that happened before today
- *http://api.joind.in/v2.1/events?filter=cfp* for events with a Call for Papers currently open

Notice that the URLs are *not* along the lines of */events/sortBy/Past* or any other format that puts extra variables in the URL, but they use query variables instead. This data set, in both cases, still utilizes the */events/* collection, but sorted and/or filtered accordingly.

Resource Structure and Hypermedia

Exactly how the resource is returned can vary hugely; REST doesn't dictate how to structure the representations sent. For example, a GitHub gist in JSON format looks like this:

```
{
  "url": "https://api.github.com/gists/17018bf64b89dd179322",
  "forks_url": "https://api.github.com/gists/17018bf64b89dd179322/forks",
  "commits_url": "https://api.github.com/gists/17018bf64b89dd179322/commits",
```

```json
  "id": "17018bf64b89dd179322",
  "git_pull_url": "https://gist.github.com/17018bf64b89dd179322.git",
  "git_push_url": "https://gist.github.com/17018bf64b89dd179322.git",
  "html_url": "https://gist.github.com/17018bf64b89dd179322",
  "files": {
    "text.txt": {
      "filename": "text.txt",
      "type": "text/plain",
      "language": "Text",
      "raw_url": "https://gist.githubusercontent.com/lornajane/
17018bf64b89dd179322/raw/336516c8e23e55265245bf589ae56aafa9cbbcf2/text.txt",
      "size": 18,
      "truncated": false,
      "content": "Some riveting text"
    }
  },
  "public": true,
  "created_at": "2015-07-23T18:30:57Z",
  "updated_at": "2015-07-23T18:30:57Z",
  "description": "Gist created by API",
  "comments": 0,
  "user": null,
  "comments_url": "https://api.github.com/gists/17018bf64b89dd179322/comments",
  "owner": {
    "login": "lornajane",
    "id": 172607,
    "avatar_url": "https://avatars.githubusercontent.com/u/172607?v=3",
    "gravatar_id": "",
    "url": "https://api.github.com/users/lornajane",
    "html_url": "https://github.com/lornajane",
    "followers_url": "https://api.github.com/users/lornajane/followers",
    "following_url": "https://api.github.com/users/lornajane/
following{/other_user}",
    "gists_url": "https://api.github.com/users/lornajane/gists{/gist_id}",
    "starred_url": "https://api.github.com/users/lornajane/
starred{/owner}{/repo}",
    "subscriptions_url": "https://api.github.com/users/lornajane/subscriptions",
    "organizations_url": "https://api.github.com/users/lornajane/orgs",
    "repos_url": "https://api.github.com/users/lornajane/repos",
    "events_url": "https://api.github.com/users/lornajane/events{/privacy}",
    "received_events_url": "https://api.github.com/users/lornajane/
received_events",
    "type": "User",
    "site_admin": false
  },
  "forks": [

  ],
  "history": [
    {
      "user": {
        "login": "lornajane",
```

```
      "id": 172607,
      "avatar_url": "https://avatars.githubusercontent.com/u/172607?v=3",
      "gravatar_id": "",
      "url": "https://api.github.com/users/lornajane",
      "html_url": "https://github.com/lornajane",
      "followers_url": "https://api.github.com/users/lornajane/followers",
      "following_url": "https://api.github.com/users/lornajane/
      following{/other_user}",
      "gists_url": "https://api.github.com/users/lornajane/gists{/gist_id}",
      "starred_url": "https://api.github.com/users/lornajane/
      starred{/owner}{/repo}",
      "subscriptions_url": "https://api.github.com/users/lornajane/
      subscriptions",
      "organizations_url": "https://api.github.com/users/lornajane/orgs",
      "repos_url": "https://api.github.com/users/lornajane/repos",
      "events_url": "https://api.github.com/users/lornajane/events{/privacy}",
      "received_events_url": "https://api.github.com/users/lornajane/
received_events",
      "type": "User",
      "site_admin": false
    },
    "version": "0392fec1b0a32463ec005942fb088aae6c47a763",
    "committed_at": "2015-07-23T18:30:57Z",
    "change_status": {
      "total": 1,
      "additions": 1,
      "deletions": 0
    },
    "url": "https://api.github.com/gists/
17018bf64b89dd179322/0392fec1b0a32463ec005942fb088aae6c47a763"
    }
  ]
}
```

Whereas a talk from Joind.in, also in JSON, would look like this:

```
{
    "talks": [
        {
            "talk_title": "Everything You Ever Wanted to Know About Deployment
But Were Afraid to Ask",
            "talk_description": "Deployment can be a real bugbear for many web
developers. From building something easy to deploy and manage; to coming up
with a repeatable, consistent process; to continuous deployment...deployment
can keep you up at night for months on end. In this talk I'll cover the follow
ing topics:\n- The deployment maturity model\n- How to build a deployable appli
cation, from technology choice to instrumentation\n- Deployment velocity: Why
your process matters more than how often you deploy\n- Deployment tools and pro
cesses: How to automate your troubles away\n- CI/Automated testing: Know you're
deploying something good, or at least how worried you should be about it\n- Auto
mated testing vs monitoring: How they converge\n- When are you ready to deploy
continuously? How do you make the jump?",
            "start_date": "2012-11-08T13:00:00-05:00",
```

```
            "average_rating": 5,
            "comments_enabled": 1,
            "comment_count": 4,
            "speakers": [
                {
                    "speaker_name": "Laura Thomson",
                    "speaker_uri": "http://api.joind.in/v2.1/users/20041"
                }
            ],
            "tracks": [],
            "uri": "http://api.joind.in/v2.1/talks/7660",
            "verbose_uri": "http://api.joind.in/v2.1/talks/7660?verbose=yes",
            "website_uri": "http://joind.in/talk/view/7660",
            "comments_uri": "http://api.joind.in/v2.1/talks/7660/comments",
            "verbose_comments_uri": "http://api.joind.in/v2.1/talks/7660/
comments?verbose=yes",
            "event_uri": "http://api.joind.in/v2.1/events/1056"
        }
    ],
    "meta": {
        "count": 1,
        "this_page": "http://api.joind.in/v2.1/talks/7660?start=0&resultsper
page=20"
    }
}
```

The two formats are quite different, and in fact the fields and formats available in a RESTful service will differ between each and every kind of service you could wish to encounter. But there are some common features, as can be seen even from this small sample size. Both responses include some nested information and some links out to other resources or collections. The decisions you make around handling data formats and versioning your API are a topic in their own right and covered in Chapter 12.

Build the Basic RESTful Server

REST makes the most of HTTP's best features, placing all the metadata about the request and response into the headers, and reserving the main body of the communications for the actual content. This means that a correctly implemented RESTful service will make use of verbs, status codes, and headers so that all the extra information goes in the "envelope" of the request, and only the content is in the body. See Appendix A and Appendix B for tables of common status codes and headers.

Example Project: The Wishlist

Since it's always easier to be shown than told, I've created a very tiny example RESTful service to use as an example, less than a hundred lines of PHP code in a single file (and a separate storage class that you can find on the GitHub repo)! We'll use this to show the concepts in very plain PHP and see a simple service in action, then move on and discuss the options for real-world RESTful implementations in PHP.

This particular example just allows us to add items to a wishlist, giving them a name and linking to where that product can be found online. As I mentioned, there's a very simple storage class that just writes to CSV behind the scenes, so if you want to pull the code from this book's accompanying repository and try it for yourself, it should work regardless of your plaform. The basic structure of the wishlist example project is shown in Example 8-1.

Example 8-1. Basic structure of my one-file RESTful service

```php
<?php

require("ItemStorage.php");

set_exception_handler(function ($e) {
  $code = $e->getCode() ?: 400;
  header("Content-Type: application/json", NULL, $code);
  echo json_encode(["error" => $e->getMessage()]);
  exit;
});

// assume JSON, handle requests by verb and path
$verb = $_SERVER['REQUEST_METHOD'];
$url_pieces = explode('/', $_SERVER['PATH_INFO']);
$storage = new ItemStorage();

// catch this here, we don't support many routes yet
if($url_pieces[1] != 'items') {
  throw new Exception('Unknown endpoint', 404);
}

switch($verb) {
  case 'GET':
    ...
    break;
  // two cases so similar we'll just share code
  case 'POST':
  case 'PUT':
    ...
    break;
  case 'DELETE':
    ...
  default:
    throw new Exception('Method Not Supported', 405);
}

// this is the output handler
```

```
header("Content-Type: application/json");
echo json_encode($data);
```

Looking at the structure, there are a few elements there that are quite important in RESTful services and that are worth a mention. First, there's the ItemStorage class that just hides all the CSV and array manipulation so that we can concentrate on the RESTful elements.

The exception handler is declared nice and early and importantly, it is output-format aware. It is very frustrating for users when a service that should usually return JSON or XML suddenly returns HTML when an error occurs. Much better practice is to return in the expected data format even when there is an error. This example service just assumes you want JSON, but in Chapter 3 we discussed content negotiation and for a service that supports multiple response formats, it is best to parse those headers and work out what that preferred output format is as soon as possible so that the exception handler can return it if anything goes wrong.

In a RESTful service, the action that is performed by the service is dependent hugely on the verb in use so that's parsed out. It will also be necessary to know which URL was actually accessed, and usually we inspect the individual pieces of a URL so that is parsed here. Beware that depending on your web server and rewrite rule setup, you may need to use $_SERVER[REQUEST_URI] rather than $_SERVER[PATH_INFO]. There's also a little check here since our application will only support requests to /items, so anything else we just throw the Exception and let the exception handler return a sensible format. Notice that this includes the correct status code to return—it is entirely not acceptable to return a 200 when things did not go well! Status codes are important in REST and you'll see them used with all our examples as we work through them.

The only other thing to mention before we look at the individual verbs is the two lines at the end of the file. Technically this is the "output handler," where our application will translate the return data to the correct format (recursively if required) and return it with the correct headers. For this case where we're assuming JSON, it's pretty straightforward, as you can see. Making sure that *all* output goes through common handlers is a great way of ensuring consistent formats and also making sure that elements such as metadata, hypermedia, and other touches are correct everywhere. This makes maintaining your API, and potentially adding a new data format in the future, much less painful.

There are some mysterious blank patches in this example code that we'll move on to inspect by visiting each verb in turn.

Create Resources with POST

Resources are created by making a POST request to the collection to which the new resource will belong. The body of the request will contain a representation of the new resource, with the Content-Type header set appropriately so that the server will know how to understand it. When the resource has been successfully created, a successful status code will be included with the response.

It's common to choose a status code of 201 (which means "Created") when a new resource has been made, and to either return a representation of the new resource in the body, or to set a Location header, redirecting the consumer to the URI of the new record. It's also perfectly valid to return either a 202 "Accepted" (but not completed) status code or a 200 "OK"—and it's also helpful to return a representation of the resource (appropriately formatted according to the Accept header) including information about the URI of this new item.

In the event that the resource cannot be created, an informative status code and error message should be returned to the user. In general, a 400 "Bad Request" status code would be appropriate for a request that either wasn't understood, or didn't pass validation rules. If a response can't be served in a format understood by the client, then 406 "Not Acceptable" would be appropriate to indicate a content negotiation problem. There are also a very large number of other status codes (*http://bit.ly/wiki-status-codes*) to choose from (see Appendix A for a handy list), depending on what exactly went wrong.

In the wishlist example application, the code for a request made with the POST verb is so similar to the code needed for PUT that they are combined. The result is shown in Example 8-2.

Example 8-2. Example code for creating and updating resources in the example wishlist application

```
case 'POST':
case 'PUT':
  // read the JSON
  $params = json_decode(file_get_contents("php://input"), true);
  if(!$params) {
    throw new Exception("Data missing or invalid");
  }
  if($verb == 'PUT') {
    $id = $url_pieces[2];
    $item = $storage->update($id, $params);
    $status = 204;
  } else {
    $item = $storage->create($params);
    $status = 201;
  }
```

```
    $storage->save();

    // send header, avoid output handler
    header("Location: " . $item['url'], null,$status);
    exit;
    break;
```

The code snippet here first reads the php://input stream, which is the raw body of the request as it came in. We use this when working with JSON since the $_POST functionality only works on form data. First, the incoming data is put through json_decode() and then checked—if the data is missing or if the JSON wasn't valid then this will return false and we throw an Exception.

To keep the code short, there's a lack of validation before we pass the data through to the ItemStorage class to create a new record and then to save it. The correct response when creating a record successfully is to return a 201 "Created" status and offer a redirect in the shape of a Location header to point to where the newly created resource can be found.

If I call this with cURL on the command line, you can see the request and response in Example 8-3 and observe all of this in action.

Example 8-3. Create a new resource on the RESTful wishlist service using cURL

```
$ curl -v -X POST -H "Content-Type: application/json" http://localhost:8080/
rest.php/items --data '{"link": "http://www.amazon.co.uk/dp/B00FWRIAUS/","name":
"notebook"}'
* Connected to localhost (127.0.0.1) port 8080 (#0)
> POST /rest.php/items HTTP/1.1
> User-Agent: curl/7.38.0
> Host: localhost:8080
> Accept: */*
> Content-Type: application/json
> Content-Length: 69
>
* upload completely sent off: 69 out of 69 bytes
< HTTP/1.1 201 Created
< Host: localhost:8080
< Connection: close
< X-Powered-By: PHP/5.6.4-4ubuntu6
< Location: http://localhost:8080/rest.php/items/dd44d
< Content-type: text/html; charset=UTF-8
<
* Closing connection 0
```

First, look at the request I made. It's a POST request and I also included the Content-Type header since I'm sending JSON in the body. This example API assumes JSON, but it is good practice to check that the expected data format arrives, or even to accept more than one format, in which case you will need to read the headers to make sure you know how to interpret the body.

My command also includes the -v switch to cURL, which makes it show the headers in the request and response in addition to the response body that it would normally show. This is *very* useful when working with RESTful APIs as there are a few scenarios (including this one where we create data) where you may not get body data returned but there is important information in the status code or headers.

The data should include a link field and a name field, so those are placed here in JSON. I constructed this simple data packet by hand, but you could easily have PHP do this for you. If you run into issues with generating valid JSON, try checking your data with the jsonlint.com website, which is a very handy tool.

The response comes back with a 201 "Created" status code so I know that my item has been successfully added to the collection. To fetch the item itself, I can follow the Location header in the response. Some APIs will also return the resource in the body of the response and that's also valid. We refer to resources by their URIs; with that information, we can operate on this resource as we wish.

An alternative approach to using POST on a collection to create a new resource is appropriate in the situation when the consumer, rather than the server, sets the identifier of the new record. In this scenario, the representation of the new resource can instead be sent in a PUT request directly to the new URI. Care must be taken, when designing a system like this, to ensure that multiple consumers do not pick the same URIs, either causing conflicts or overwrites. At least make sure that these are dealt with in a sane way, perhaps using the 409 status code, which means "Conflict."

Fetch a Resource or Collection with GET

To fetch representations of resources, use the GET verb applied to either a collection or an individual resource without sending any body content with the GET request. The resources will usually appear with exactly the same structure, regardless of whether they were requested within a collection or on their own. The status code will be 200 if the record(s) were successfully retrieved, although other "good" status codes may also be used here such as 302 "Found" or 304 "Not Modified" (more about caching in the next section when we discuss how to update records).

If, however, the record isn't successfully found, a status code describing the problem will be returned. In a vast number of cases, this will be a 404 status code, to indicate that the record wasn't found or doesn't exist. If the user isn't authenticated, a 401 "Not Authorized" status code may be returned; a user who has identified herself but doesn't have permission to see this item may receive a 403 "Forbidden" instead. Any one of a number of other possible failure cases could also occur, and these should have the appropriate status codes associated with them.

The code for fetching either one or many records in our example wishlist service is quite simple, so we'll view it all at once:

```
case 'GET':
  if(isset($url_pieces[2])) {
    try {
      $data = $storage->getOne($url_pieces[2]);
    } catch (UnexpectedValueException $e) {
      throw new Exception("Resource does not exist", 404);
    }
  } else {
    $data = $storage->getAll();
  }
  break;
```

The check for the `$url_pieces[2]` variable is to allow us to distinguish between two types of URL:

- *http://localhost:8080/rest.php/items* to get all the resources in the collection
- *http://localhost:8080/rest.php/items/dd44d* for fetching a single resource

If we only want a specific resource, then we ask the storage class for it, and if we can't find it then we throw an exception so that the exception handler can return a sane message and importantly the correct status code to the user. If we want all the resources in a collection, then we just grab everything and this then goes out through the output handler. Similarly, a successfully found single resource is correctly formatted and returned by the output handler we already discussed.

Let's look at examples of finding a record using cURL. These examples also use the Python JSON module for formatting, a technique which we'll look at in more detail in Chapter 11.

First, the collection (so we can see which individual resources are available for us to pick):

```
$ curl -s http://localhost:8080/rest.php/items | python -mjson.tool
[
    {
        "link": "http://www.amazon.co.uk/My-First-Baby-Annabell-Doll/dp/
B00FBWB9A2",
        "name": "doll",
        "url": "http://localhost:8080/rest.php/items/ed6f1"
    },
    {
        "link": "http://www.amazon.co.uk/dp/B00FWRIAUS/",
        "name": "notebook",
        "url": "http://localhost:8080/rest.php/items/b4fa2"
    },
    {
        "link": "http://www.amazon.co.uk/dp/B00MA3I0BG",
```

```
        "name": "travel organiser",
        "url": "http://localhost:8080/rest.php/items/7f868"
    },
    {

        "link": "http://www.amazon.co.uk/dp/B00FWRIAUS/",
        "name": "notebook",
        "url": "http://localhost:8080/rest.php/items/dd44d"
    }
]
```

And picking an individual record from the list (the notebook we added earlier):

```
$ curl -s http://localhost:8080/rest.php/items/dd44d | python -mjson.tool
{
    "link": "http://www.amazon.co.uk/dp/B00FWRIAUS/",
    "name": "notebook",
    "url": "http://localhost:8080/rest.php/items/dd44d"
}
```

The resources return the same *representation* whether they are fetched by themselves or in the collection, which is a key element of RESTful services. It's also important to note that the resource includes information on how to represent itself, here using the url field. We'll talk more about data formats in Chapter 12, but it's important to note here that for service to be RESTful, information about how to reach a single resource should always be provided.

How about when a resource doesn't exist? It's important to consider failure cases as well as successful ones, and here's how we handle that:

```
$ curl -v http://localhost:8080/rest.php/items/nonsense
* Connected to localhost (127.0.0.1) port 8080 (#0)
> GET /rest.php/items/nonsense HTTP/1.1
> User-Agent: curl/7.38.0
> Host: localhost:8080
> Accept: */*
>
< HTTP/1.1 404 Not Found
< Host: localhost:8080
< Connection: close
< X-Powered-By: PHP/5.6.4-4ubuntu6
< Content-Type: application/json
<
* Closing connection 0
{"error":"Resource does not exist"}
```

I requested a resource that I knew didn't exist and the API correctly returns a 404 status code. There is also an error message in the body of the response, which is a good opportunity to give more detail on an error (but don't be tempted to put status information here!). There are some great standards for describing errors (including, for example, the SOAPFault responses), and similar standards are now being used with

---

RESTful services; see Chapter 12 for examples of these standards and a discussion of how to implement them.

If your API implements rate limiting, then it might be that the resource exists and the user has permission to see it, but she has exceeded her allotted number of requests in a given time frame. In this situation, either a 420 "Enhance Your Calm" or 429 "Too Many Requests" would be a good status to return.

Some APIs (this includes GitHub) will return a 404 to indicate that the record exists but the requesting user does not have access to it. This makes it impossible to deduce the existence (or nonexistence) of a record without the rights to see it! Exposing such details is known as "leaking information" and in many settings it is something of which to be wary.

Update a Resource with PUT

To edit records RESTfully is a multistep process. First, the resource should be retrieved by GET. Then, the representation of the resource can be altered as needed, and that resource should be PUT back to its original URI. Even if only a small part of the record needs to be changed, REST deals with representations of resources, so the whole resource will be fetched and sent back for the update. Identical to when a resource was created using POST, the PUT request will include the resource representation in the body and the appropriate Content-Type in the header.

In the example application, the POST and GET examples have already been shown. Next, we can take that data and update it using a PUT request. In this trivially simple example, the code for PUT and POST is so similar that I placed them both in the same example, Example 8-2.

To see this code in action, here's an example that updates the record we created earlier:

```
$ curl -v -X PUT -H "Content-Type: application/json" http://localhost:8080/
rest.php/items/dd44d --data '{"link": "http://www.amazon.co.uk/dp/
B00FWRIAUS/","name": "awesome notebook"}'
* Connected to localhost (127.0.0.1) port 8080 (#0)
> PUT /rest.php/items/dd44d HTTP/1.1
> User-Agent: curl/7.38.0
> Host: localhost:8080
> Accept: */*
> Content-Type: application/json
> Content-Length: 77
>
* upload completely sent off: 77 out of 77 bytes
< HTTP/1.1 204 No Content
< Host: localhost:8080
< Connection: close
< X-Powered-By: PHP/5.6.4-4ubuntu6
```

```
< Location: http://localhost:8080/rest.php/items/dd44d
< Content-type: text/html; charset=UTF-8
<
* Closing connection 0
```

The curl command shows my PUT request and includes the Content-Type header, the -v switch, and some JSON content, much like the POST example earlier. The main differences are the verb we use and also the fact that this time, the PUT request operates on a specific resource rather than requesting a new resource be created in a collection.

When updating a record, it's quite common to include some identifying information for the contents of the resource, such as a Last-Modified header or an ETag, to allow us to check whether the resource changed as a result of something else between the GET and PUT, as this isn't an atomic operation. This is closely linked to how cacheable different URIs are, which we covered in "Caching Headers" on page 37.

For a newcomer to REST, updating a representation of a whole resource can seem cumbersome when only a tiny part of it is actually changing, but don't be tempted to diverge from this approach and break the RESTfulness of the design. If it really does seem like an alternative approach would be better, then you have two options: either create a subresource or use the PATCH verb.

Creating a subresource is simplest, if you want to change one field of a resource, and make that field available at its own URI. For example, if it seems like overkill to update a whole user record just to change an email address, then instead create a resource /user/42/email. This smaller resource can then be subject to GET, change, and PUT instead of fetching and then pushing back a whole user profile.

The alternative is to use PATCH to make a small change to an existing record. This is becoming more widely implemented and supported, and you'll see examples in the GitHub API that has been used as an example elsewhere in this book. GitHub allows the user to make changes to individual fields in a record by supplying the data you want to change and making a PATCH request instead of a PUT request to the existing resource's URI.

DELETE a Resource

This is the most damaging move, but it's also the simplest. The DELETE verb is sent with a request to the URI of the item to be deleted, with no body content necessary. Many services will return 200 for "OK"—or simply a 204 for "No Content"—when an item was successfully deleted, and a 404 "Not Found" if the item didn't exist. However, if the request was made to delete something, and the record doesn't exist, many services see that as "success" and will return 200 or 204, regardless of what really happened (unless the record couldn't be deleted for some reason, such as the user does not have the proper permission). This idea of always behaving in the same way each time the action is called is known as *idempotency* and is expected behavior for both GET and DELETE requests.

Our example wishlist service also offers DELETE (it's up to you whether you actually delete a record or just set a deleted property and avoid returning it in future; this is just about the outward-facing implementation) and the PHP code is shown in Example 8-4.

Example 8-4. Example wishlist service handling a DELETE request in PHP

```php
case 'DELETE':
    $id = $url_pieces[2];
    $storage->remove($id);
    $storage->save();
    header("Location: http://localhost:8080/items", null, 204);
    exit;
    break;
```

All that happens here is that we work out which item we're getting a DELETE request for, and then we ask the storage class to remove that and save itself. The 204 status code is just to let the client know that there is no content to return, and while there is also a Location header, this is entirely optional as the client will probably know where it wants to go next.

The DELETE method in action looks the same whether the resource existed or not:

```
$ curl -X DELETE -v http://localhost:8080/rest.php/items/958a9
* Connected to localhost (127.0.0.1) port 8080 (#0)
> DELETE /rest.php/items/958a9 HTTP/1.1
> User-Agent: curl/7.38.0
> Host: localhost:8080
> Accept: */*
>
< HTTP/1.1 204 No Content
< Host: localhost:8080
< Connection: close
< X-Powered-By: PHP/5.6.4-4ubuntu6
< Location: http://localhost:8080/items
< Content-type: text/html; charset=UTF-8
<
* Closing connection 0
```

In many ways DELETE is much simpler than the PUT, PATCH, or DELETE methods since it does not include body data (and should not include body data). After deleting the resource, our service will return a 404 if it is requested again.

RESTful Versus Useful

REST is truly an elegant way to build services, and a nice way to work with data over HTTP. Not every application has requirements that are best met by a RESTful service, so don't be tempted to make architectural decisions based on the current fashionable technologies. Standards are always an excellent thing to follow; they've been created by people who have implemented this several times and learned from their mistakes. That said, don't be afraid to break the rules just as you would for any other architectural decision in software engineering. Many APIs are criticized because they are deemed "not RESTful." While I recommend that you follow the strategies in this chapter, it's acceptable for you to take inspiration from REST, rather than implementing it to the letter. Do make sure, though, that your API is still well documented, robust, and, most of all, useful.

CHAPTER 9

Webhooks

Webhooks are becoming an increasingly popular way of enabling other applications to integrate with yours, and they flip the traditional API model on its head. Rather than requesting the data from the API provider at the time that the consumer needs the information, the webhook on the provider notifies consumers when an event of interest occurs. While this is a little more complicated to implement in your application than just offering the ability to fetch data in machine-readable format, it can be an excellent solution for event-driven use cases. It also reduces the load of having many API clients polling a server to check for updates, since the server itself can just send out notifications when relevant events occur.

A good example of when to use a webhook could be when adding new comments to an article or photo. In order to show that comment data elsewhere, another system would need to keep polling for updates; by using a webhook instead, no polling is needed. The second system simply registers an endpoint that the information about a new comment should be sent to. When a comment is made, the first application sends information about the comment to all the other applications that requested to receive it.

The overall idea of webhooks could be respresented along the lines shown in Figure 9-1.

When an event occurs, the server processes the event, and sends information about the event to any third party that has registered an interest in being notified about the event. Those webhooks may update a news feed, send emails, store information to a database, announce the event into a chat channel...or something else. Usually the webhook will consist of a POST request to an endpoint that you nominate, with a body that contains all the relevant data and representations of all affected records. You may still need to make some additional API calls to fetch related data, but often all the critical information needed to stay informed is included in the webhook.

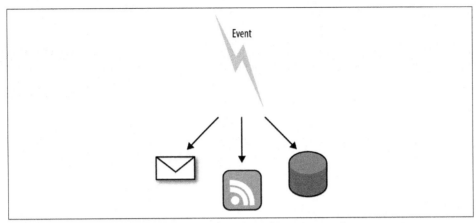

Figure 9-1. One event being passed to a number of listening applications

If this reminds you strongly of the Publish-Subscribe or Observer design patterns, that isn't a surprise, as it fits exactly that use case. The application allows interested parties to register themselves as needing to be informed when an event occurs or something changes. When that event does occur, it sends notification using the webhook.

GitHub's Webhooks

The webhook functionality that I probably use the most is GitHub's. They have a great API that you've seen examples of in Chapter 8 and Chapter 5 already, so it isn't a surprise that their webhook features are also very good. GitHub itself also benefits hugely from offering webhooks, as they are very widely used by programmers: imagine if every continuous integration server in the world pinged GitHub's API every minute! That would require a lot of server capacity even when there is no new data to return.

Receivers of webhooks are usually continuous integration platforms such as Jenkins or TravisCI, and I often use a Hubot (*http://hubot.github.com*) (GitHub's open source chatbot), which will notify a chat channel that a commit has been made or a comment added to a pull request. The possibilities are endless, so let's look at a simple example of setting up a webhook and getting some data from it.

On GitHub, you can configure a webhook to be per-repository or per-organization, depending on whether you want to be notified of events on just one of your repositories or have the same webhook apply to all of them; the per-organization option is very handy if you have a lot of repositories. You can configure multiple webhooks for each organization or repository and you also have a choice of what they respond to.

When adding a new webhook to a repository, a screen like that in Figure 9-2 appears.

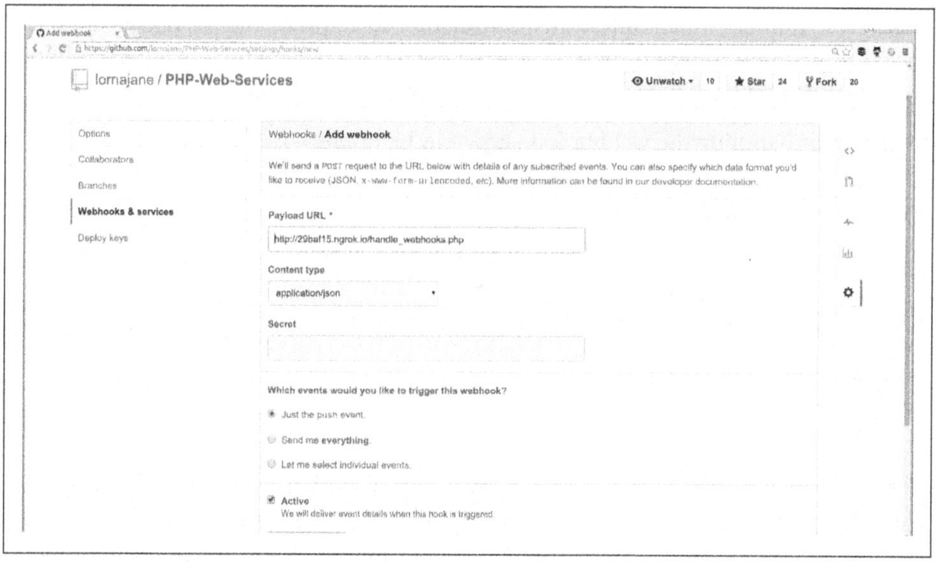

Figure 9-2. Configuring a GitHub webhook

You can see an example of the data that will be sent for each type of event by checking the documentation (*https://developer.github.com/webhooks/*). Depending on the event, this can be quite verbose, as it will include information about the author, any committers, the repository itself, and so on.

In the example, you can see that we can set an endpoint that the webhook should deliver its payload to. The file *handle_webhooks.php* is on my local development machine, so in order to allow the GitHub webhook to reach that, I'm using an ngrok tunnel. You can read more about ngrok in Chapter 10, but essentially it's a tool that opens a tunnel from your development machine to the outside world, assigns you a URL to use, and allows you to inspect the traffic going over the tunnel. I've added that URL to my webhook, and chosen to be notified of all events. Most webhooks will give you some options as to what information you are interested in, so that if you are looking for particular changes or interested in particular data, you can choose that rather than discarding the information you don't want. Along these lines, I have a tool that reports on the billable time we log through our project management tools at work; the webhook lets me configure what to receive and therefore the application knows not to send me a lot of information that I won't use or may not know how to parse.

Once the webhook is created, you'll see it listed at the bottom of the screen, and it will show a history of all the data that has been sent by this hook. It also shows whether the hook was successfully received and offers the option to retry a hook. This option to retry is invaluable when developing tools that consume webhooks and is one of the main reasons I love working with the GitHub API so much. In this case I'm also using the ngrok tunnel, which offers inspection of the request and response, and also includes the same ability to replay a request, which is really handy for other webhook sources that might not have all the tooling support that GitHub offers.

My code for handling the webhook is shown in Example 9-1.

Example 9-1. Webhook-handling code

```php
<?php

$data = json_decode(file_get_contents("php://input"), true);

file_put_contents("example_webhook.txt", print_r($data, true));

echo $data['zen'];
```

The first line actually does multiple things; let's start at the deepest level inside the parentheses. We call `file_get_contents()` on the `php://input` stream; we've seen this in previous examples and it simply reads in the raw body of the incoming POST request (use this stream with PUT requests as well in RESTful services). We use this rather than `$_POST` because the webhooks are often in JSON or XML format rather than the form post that PHP's `$_POST` superglobal expects. Now that we've got the content of the POST request body, it's passed to `json_decode()` as the first parameter. That second parameter to `json_encode()` simply returns the result as an array rather than the default object, which I find easier to work with. The resulting array is then assigned to `$data`.

In order to inspect the data, we can simply write it to a file, which is what happens next in the example code. By passing a second parameter to `print_r()`, we cause it to return its output rather than echo it, and we then write it to the *example_webhook.txt* file. This can be a useful tactic if you need to capture the contents of an incoming hook and then put it somewhere to refer to while you build something specific that uses the data. Having an example of what you received from the previous request can be used as a handy reference.

Finally, and just for fun, this script outputs the value of the zen field, which is a little spiritual insight into your day provided by GitHub with your API response. You could access any of the data fields provided by the webhook and use them for your own purposes, but hopefully this gives you the idea.

Publishing Your Own Webhooks

If you're publishing APIs, there's no reason you shouldn't be publishing webhooks as well. We just need a little more advance setup as we need people to be able to register which hooks they want to utilize beforehand. In most cases, it makes sense to offer both webhooks and a traditional API so that you can update consumers on events that have just happened, as well as allow them to access other data as needed.

Webhooks are fired in response to something happening, so they usually appear in code after a specific event is detected and handled, similar to where you would put the code in charge of sending an email notification, for example. To give you a very simple outline, I've created Example 9-2, which takes a form and then just POSTs the data to any interested parties.

Example 9-2. Code receives a form, and sends out a webhook

```php
<?php

$hook_endpoints = ["http://29baf15.ngrok.io/handle_webhooks.php",
    "http://localhost:8080/handle_webhooks.php"];

if($_POST) {
    // very lazily chuck the whole thing at json_encode
    // a Real Application would validate or look things up
    $post_body = json_encode($_POST);

    // send using streams
    $context = stream_context_create([
        'http' => [
            'method'  => 'POST',
            'header'  => 'Content-Type: application/json',
            'content' => $post_body,
        ]
    ]);

    foreach ($hook_endpoints as $endpoint) {
        $success = file_get_contents($endpoint, false, $context);

        echo "<p>Send to:" . $endpoint . "</p>\n";
    }

    include ("hook_thanks.html");
} else {
    // display the template
    include("hook_form.html");
}
```

We start with a spot of initialization, creating an array of the endpoints to which we should webhook. Then there is a check to see if we received any POST data; if not then the input template is displayed. If there is data, then we simply turn it all into JSON, and POST it as a webhook to each endpoint in turn, using PHP's stream handling.

In a more complicated application, it might be appropriate to first process the form data in some way, such as to update a record. Once that has been done, it is common to send a webhook that contains the new state of the resource, often including nested/related data, and sometimes including information about which fields changed and maybe even their previous values. When building your own webhooks it is very important to consider what your end users will actually want to achieve, so that you can design your webhooks to include the right amount of data. Along the same lines, I'd recommend offering to consumers some configuration of which webhook events to subscribe to.

The example here shows a webhook which is architecturally stuck at the end of a controller, after the data has been processed and before we return a response; it is comparable to sending an email notification of something happening on the system. This is an easy place to put the webhook and makes this example easy to follow, but there are some alternatives that are worth examining.

In a real application, we probably don't want to wait for someone's webhook endpoint to respond before we complete our own request. The email-sending analogy also bears out here as it's unusual nowadays to send email synchronously from web applications. A better approach for either webhooks or email sending is to use a job queue and simply create a job with all the data required to send the email or hook. Your application can then essentially "forget" about the additional task as the queue will take care of it in due course. Detailed discussion of job queues are out of the scope of this chapter but a tool such as beanstalkd (*https://kr.github.io/beanstalkd/*) or gearman (*http://gearman.org*) would be a good place to start if you want to add something like this to your own applications.

Whether you webhook on all actions, or just offer a few notifications in your application, take care to consider the use cases from the consumer's point of view, and also think about how you can include these in your application. This chapter has shown you some examples of working webhooks, plus an example and discussion of how to design and build your own. As this style of integration between systems becomes increasingly common, I expect more and more of our PHP applications to include features like this.

CHAPTER 10

HTTP Tools

This book began with an introduction to HTTP that included simple tools such as cURL and HTTPie (see "Command-Line HTTP" on page 6 for examples). These are key tools that you'll see used again and again throughout the book, but there are also a host of other tools which are very handy in particular scenarios; this chapter is dedicated to showing you the other tools in the box.

These are all tools that you can use without changing your application (although we'll talk about that too, in Chapter 11) so you can quickly inspect traffic in a variety of settings and review what's happening.

We'll start with cURL and HTTPie, and add in two tools that I use extensively when working with JSON services in particular: jq and the Python JSON module. There are also some excellent GUI alternatives to these command-line tools that may fit your needs better. We'll look at Postman, which is a great graphical tool for working with web requests.

On a more network level, there's Wireshark, an excellent tool for inspecting traffic as it goes over your network card. There's ngrok, which allows you to make your local API or website visible externally; I use this regularly when working with local development APIs and with webhooks. We'll also look at the proxy tools Charles and Fiddler.

Each of these tools will help you to solve different problems, so it's well worth taking a look at each of them. That way, you'll know what's available and where to start when you need to use these tools in your own work.

Easy Command-Line JSON

The trouble with JSON APIs is that they often return a wall of text; some APIs offer pretty printing but otherwise the result is really not designed for humans to read. An example would be something like Example 10-1, which is a simple request to get a list of Pinterest boards for a specific user.

 To use the Pinterest API, you'll need to register an account with Pinterest and then get an access token. They support standard OAuth, but there's also a handy access token generator (*https://dev.pinterest.com/tools/access_token/*), which is the quickest way to get started with these examples.

Example 10-1. Unformatted JSON from the Pinterest API

```
$ curl https://api.pinterest.com/v1/me/boards/ -H 'Authorization: Bearer AVHk...A'
{"data": [{"url": "https://www.pinterest.com/lorna0641/crochet/", "id":
"346636571258417680", "name": "crochet"}, {"url": "https://www.pinterest.com/
lorna0641/wood/", "id": "346636571258417677", "name": "wood"}, {"url": "https://
www.pinterest.com/lorna0641/sew/", "id": "346636571258417679", "name": "sew"}]}
```

There are a few things we can do to make this easier to read than the output we get from cURL. One option is to simply use HTTPie, which will parse the JSON and present it in a much prettier format, as you can see in Example 10-2.

Example 10-2. JSON output from HTTPie calling the Pinterest API

```
$ http -p b https://api.pinterest.com/v1/me/boards/ 'Authorization:Bearer AVHk...A'
{
    "data": [
        {
            "id": "346636571258417680",
            "name": "crochet",
            "url": "https://www.pinterest.com/lorna0641/crochet/"
        },
        {
            "id": "346636571258417677",
            "name": "wood",
            "url": "https://www.pinterest.com/lorna0641/wood/"
        },
        {
            "id": "346636571258417679",
            "name": "sew",
            "url": "https://www.pinterest.com/lorna0641/sew/"
        }
    ]
}
```

When investigating a new API or working closely with a particular endpoint, it's always worth checking if there is a built-in "pretty print" mode. Many APIs offer this and it can be valuable when a human needs to inspect the output. I'd also recommend this feature as an excellent thing to consider adding to your own APIs.

There are also JSON-specific tools that I use with cURL to output the JSON in a more readable way. These tools also have a side advantage in that they are designed to work with any JSON data that you have, not just with web requests.

One nice option is to just pipe your JSON through the Python JSON module from cURL. I use this a lot since it's usually available if you have Python installed, which I do. To add this to a `curl` command, only two things need to change:

- Add the `-s` switch to your `curl` command to suppress the progress output, since this will confuse things.
- Pipe the output of cURL to `python -mjson.tool`.

Another tool that is a bit more featured is the excellent jq (*https://stedolan.github.io/jq/*). This does a great deal more than just pretty-print your JSON, but that's mostly what I use it for! It's available for easy install on most platforms (it's included in my package manager on Ubuntu, for example) and is recommended if you work regularly with JSON.

The commands to pipe cURL output through to other processors are pretty similar and I think it helps to see them side by side.

First, the original `curl` command again:

```
curl https://api.pinterest.com/v1/me/boards/ -H 'Authorization: Bearer AVHk...A'
```

The next example uses the Python module:

```
curl -s https://api.pinterest.com/v1/me/boards/ -H 'Authorization: Bearer
AVHk...A' | python -mjson.tool
```

Finally, we can use jq to format the JSON nicely; the "." just tells jq to work with the entire document it receives:

```
curl -s https://api.pinterest.com/v1/me/boards/ -H 'Authorization: Bearer
AVHk...A' | jq "."
```

Any of the formatting options are great, and we also saw the HTTPie example earlier. HTTPie and jq also support color-formatted output, which can be easier to read, but this depends on your taste and also the tools easily available on your platform. Being aware of which tools are available and what they do will really help you to work efficiently with APIs of all kinds—including your own.

Graphical cURL Alternatives

Working with HTTP doesn't have to mean the command line; there are some great tools around that can do everything cURL can do, but present it in a more intuitive interface. One really excellent, cross-platform example is Postman (*https://www.getpostman.com/*). In the previous examples we looked at fetching some JSON data from an endpoint that needed an `Authorization` header. We can easily do the same with Postman; its interface is shown in Figure 10-1.

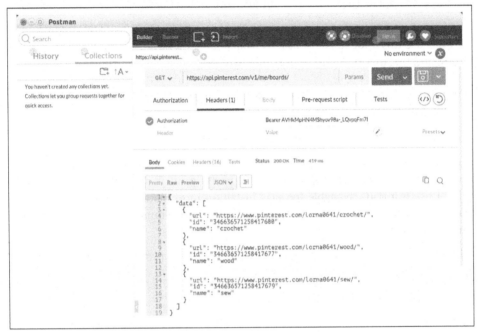

Figure 10-1. Using Postman to send HTTP requests

The main advantages of using Postman are that you can save and even group your existing requests into collections, making it easy to return to earlier examples at a later date. It is easy to change individual aspects of your request, such as the data and headers to send, without needing to edit a long command string. The output is easy to see and work with, and there are also some great time-saving features such as the ability to have Postman do your OAuth authentication steps for you when you need to fetch an access token.

There are a wide selection of tools that perform pretty similar jobs; you've seen Postman here (it started life as a Chrome plug-in but is now a standalone application in its own right), but there are others. Firefox has the HttpRequester (*http://bit.ly/ff-httpreq*) plug-in, which is very useful. On a Mac, you might also like to try Paw (*https://luckymarmot.com/paw*), which comes highly recommended.

Inspect HTTP Traffic with Wireshark

Wireshark (*http://www.wireshark.org*) is a "network protocol analyzer." In plain English, that means that it takes a copy of the traffic going over your network card, and presents it to you in a human-readable way. You don't need to do any configuration of your application or network settings to use it; once it's installed, it can just start showing us the traffic. Wireshark is cross-platform and open source.

When you run Wireshark, you see a screen like the one in Figure 10-2.

The lefthand column lets you pick which network card you want to capture (this screenshot is from my Ubuntu laptop; you'll see things a little differently on different operating systems). The "eth0" is your local wired network, "wlan0" is the wireless network, and "lo" is your local loopback. Look out for this if you're making API calls to localhost as they use "lo" rather than whatever connection your machine uses to access the outside world. If you're working with virtual machines, you will see more network connections here, so you can pick the one for which you want to see the traffic.

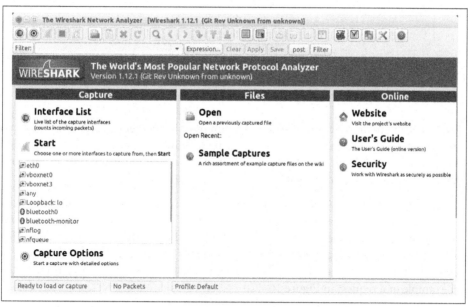

Figure 10-2. Initial screen when starting Wireshark

The other option you might want to use from this initial view is "open." Wireshark runs on your desktop or laptop and captures the traffic going over a network card on your machine. However, what if it's not your machine that you need the traffic from? It's rare to have a server with a GUI that you could install Wireshark on, so instead a command-line program called tcpdump (Windows users have a port called

WinDump) can be used. This program captures network traffic and can write it to a file; the resulting files can then be opened in Wireshark to be analyzed.

Whether the traffic is captured live or comes from a file captured elsewhere, what happens next is the same: we view the traffic and start to examine what is happening. When I start a capture on my machine, I see something like Figure 10-3.

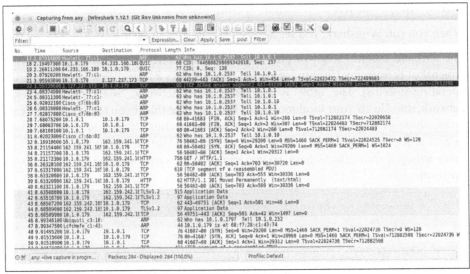

Figure 10-3. Wireshark showing all network card traffic

The first thing to do here is to restrict the amount of traffic being displayed to just the lines of interest by placing **http** in the *filter* field. Now a list of all the HTTP requests and responses that have been taking place are visible, making it possible to pick out the ones that are useful for solving a given problem.

Clicking on a request makes the detail pane open up, showing all the headers and the body of the request, or response, that was selected. This allows you to drill down and inspect all the various elements of both the body and the header of the HTTP traffic; when debugging, this is a very helpful technique for identifying whether the client is sending an incorrect request or if the problem is in the server response. You can see an example of a request in Figure 10-4.

To see the requests and responses in the context of one another, right-click on either the request or the response and choose "follow TCP stream." With this, you can clearly see the requests and responses side by side, with the request shown in red (if you're reading this in monochrome, look for a blank line separating request and response) and the response shown in blue in Figure 10-5.

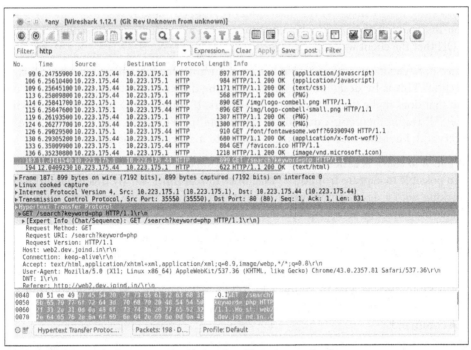

Figure 10-4. Detail of a request including headers in Wireshark

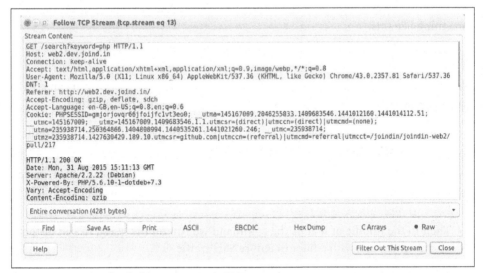

Figure 10-5. Wireshark showing a single TCP stream

Wireshark's ability to quickly show what's going on at the HTTP level without modifying the application is a huge advantage. Often, it's the first tool out of the box when something that "usually works" has suddenly stopped—and it will very quickly show you that your API is suddenly returning an HTML error message rather than the JSON that the client was expecting!

Wireshark can also handle SSL *if* it has access to the server certificate for the SSL connection. This is by design; SSL is *intended* to be difficult to intercept and report on, but that does make things tricky for developers. If you own the server that is serving the SSL traffic then you can add the certificate to Wireshark and it will be able to decrypt it, but otherwise Wireshark is unable to inspect this type of traffic.

While Wireshark is easiest to use with applications running on the same machine, it's also possible to capture from other machines in real time. Mostly this is helpful when working with a development platform that increasingly will be on a virtual machine rather than on your actual laptop.

Before you begin, you should have Wireshark installed on both the host and guest machines (on the guest machine you actually only need something called dumpcap, but I find installing Wireshark brings in the tool I need and all the dependencies). You should also be able to connect to the virtual machine via SSH; if you're using Vagrant to manage your virtual machines, you can usually do this with the vagrant ssh command.

The way this works is to run dumpcap inside the guest, and pipe the resulting data straight into Wireshark on the host machine. Since we're doing this over SSH, the command includes a filter to exclude that SSH traffic. The command therefore looks something like this:

```
wireshark -k -i <(vagrant ssh -c "sudo dumpcap -P -i any -w - -f 'not tcp port
22'" -- -ntt)
```

This is pretty complicated since there are so many moving pieces, but you can see the general shape of the command and we'll pick out the elements one at a time.

- The parentheses contain a command, the output of which we pipe to Wireshark with -k to tell it to start capturing immediately.

- The vagrant ssh command accepts a -c parameter to tell it to SSH in and immediately run the specified command. The -- and -ntt switches tell SSH to use a tty and how to read from it.

- Then in the middle of it all is the command we run on the guest, to run dumpcap on any interfaces, with a filter to ignore SSH traffic.

- Note that the dumpcap command must be run as root, which makes sense as I'd prefer it if unprivileged users did not have access to all the network traffic on a computer.

This approach means that I can run a live capture on the traffic going over the network interface of a virtual machine development platform, which is very, very useful. You can use this approach to run live capture on other machines as well, by adapting the command to use the appropriate SSH commands for the other machine you want to connect to.

Tunnel Local Traffic Remotely with ngrok

ngrok (*https://ngrok.com*) is a hosted service offering a secure tunnel for your HTTP traffic that is especially useful in a couple of specific scenarios:

- Wanting to make a local/development website or API available to the outside world, for example for testing by someone else or on a mobile device
- Wanting an external tool to be able to reach something running locally on my development platform, for example when developing webhook receivers

ngrok is cross-platform, easy to use, and can be very useful for quickly opening tunnels to endpoints that you want to share with others during development. Once ngrok is installed, it is necessary to register to use the service and obtain an authtoken. It's a one-off process to add this token to your local configuration and then everything is ready.

> The original v1 of ngrok was open source. The newer v2 is still free to use for developers but is no longer an open source tool; you will need to register an account in order to use it.

ngrok is a command-line tool that runs on a local machine and specifies which port to expose to the wider world. In this example, I'm working on a simple API endpoint (that you'll see again in Chapter 11) that is available at *http://localhost:8080* on my laptop. It's useful to be able to make this available to others, perhaps a client or a colleague in another location, and ngrok makes this very easy.

Let's start by simply exposing that port 8080 endpoint to the world using ngrok:

```
ngrok http 8080
```

This opens up a console view showing what URL the tunnel is available on, and also a simple history of the requests made. For example in Figure 10-6 you can see that my `localhost:8080` is now available on *http://29baf15.ngrok.io*. With this running, I can request that URL *http://29baf15.ngrok.io* from another device or location, and see the code running on my local machine. Under the "HTTP Requests" section, you can see the requests that were made to this endpoint, including one that failed.

```
    ⊗ – □  Terminal
ngrok by @inconshreveable                                      (Ctrl+C to quit)

Tunnel Status               online
Version                     2.0.19/2.0.19
Web Interface               http://127.0.0.1:4040
Forwarding                  http://29baf15.ngrok.io -> localhost:8080
Forwarding                  https://29baf15.ngrok.io -> localhost:8080

Connections                 ttl      opn      rt1      rt5      p50      p90
                            4        0        0.05     0.01     0.00     0.00


HTTP Requests
-------------

GET /nonsense               404 Not Found
GET /list                   200 OK
GET /list                   200 OK
GET /                       200 OK
```

Figure 10-6. ngrok tunnel in action

When the tunnel is no longer needed, simply press Ctrl-C to stop the program and close the tunnel.

ngrok also has some additional features; notice in the screenshot of the console that there is a URL labeled "Web Interface." This is a brilliant feature: it allows you to list, inspect in detail, and repeat any requests that came in to the tunnel—take a look at Figure 10-7 to see this in action using the same example shown on the console.

The web interface is split into two main sections with a list of requests on the left and the detail of the currently selected request on the righthand side of the page. The individual request can be inspected in many different ways; the default view shows the request and response but headers and raw formats are also available, which can be really useful when chasing an API problem. Especially magical in this view is the "Replay" button on the top righthand side of the detail view! Chapter 11 talks more about adding debugging into your application, but to be able to add logging or other diagnostics and very easily repeat a request that you know replicates a bug is incredibly helpful.

ngrok is a tool that I think every web developer, not specifically API developers, will find useful to have in their proverbial toolbox since it's just so useful to make your local platform reachable temporarily by others. It has other features, such as being able to register custom or reserved subdomains so that you can bring up the same development endpoints at the same places every time, so it's well worth a look.

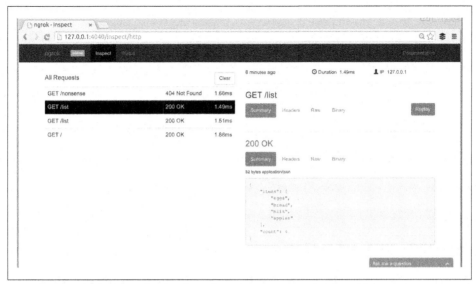

Figure 10-7. The ngrok web interface allows inspection and repeat of requests

Inspect, Edit, Repeat, and Share Requests

There are quite a few tools that provide proxy functionality and run locally on your machine, which are useful features for local API development. This section looks at two excellent tools, mitmproxy and Charles, but there are others—for example, you might want to check out Fiddler if you're on a Windows platform.

mitmproxy (*http://mitmproxy.org*) is an open source Python tool that acts as a proxy. It offers easy inspection of traffic as well as the ability to replay and change requests. It's also possible to save requests or collections of requests if you want to share a whole session, either to revisit later on or to send to colleagues or attach to an issue in an issue tracker.

mitmproxy is entirely console-based, so it's easy to run on your development machine, or on virtual machines or other servers during development. You can see it in action in Figure 10-8.

```
  ●   □  Terminal
>> GET http://api.dev.joind.in/v2.1/events?resultsperpage=6&start=0&filter=hot
        ← 200 application/json 7.21kB 95ms
   GET http://api.dev.joind.in/v2.1/events?resultsperpage=10&start=0&filter=cfp&verbose=yes
        ← 200 application/json 145B 55ms
   POST http://api.dev.joind.in/v2.1/token
         ← 200 application/json 91B 137ms
   GET http://api.dev.joind.in/v2.1/users/13?verbose=yes
        ← 200 application/json 842B 57ms
   GET http://api.dev.joind.in/v2.1/events?resultsperpage=6&start=0&filter=hot
        ← 200 application/json 7.26kB 61ms
   GET http://api.dev.joind.in/v2.1/events?resultsperpage=10&start=0&filter=cfp&verbose=yes
        ← 200 application/json 201B 51ms
   GET http://api.dev.joind.in/v2.1/events/61?verbose=yes
        ← 200 application/json 1.46kB 69ms
   POST http://api.dev.joind.in/v2.1/events/61/attending
         ← 201 application/json 66B 46ms
   GET http://api.dev.joind.in/v2.1/events/43?verbose=yes
        ← 200 application/json 2.21kB 86ms

[1/9]                                                          ?:help [*:8888]
```

Figure 10-8. mitmproxy capturing traffic

mitmproxy is very lightweight and easy to install, and will run anywhere. The project is actively developed on GitHub.

Charles (*http://www.charlesproxy.com*) is a paid-for product (a single license is $50 at the time of writing), but it's one that is absolutely invaluable, especially when working with mobile devices or when more advanced features are needed. Charles logs a list of requests and allows you to inspect them, similar to Wireshark, but it works in quite a different way since it is a true proxy, and requests are passed *through* Charles rather than the network traffic being duplicated.

Getting set up with Charles is straightforward; it automatically installs and will prompt you to install a plug-in for Firefox to enable proxying through Charles by default. If you're working with a web page making asynchronous requests, this is an excellent setup.

For those not using Firefox, you need to ask your application to proxy through Charles. Since it's common to have proxies in place, particularly on corporate networks, this is fairly easy to do on most devices; there are advanced settings when creating a network connection that will allow you to do this. You will need to enter the IP address of your machine, and the port number (8888 by default, but you can change it in the proxy settings in Charles) into the proxy settings fields when creating and editing the network settings. When a new device starts proxying through your machine, you'll get an alert from Charles that lets you allow or deny access.

Once everything is up and running, click on the "Sequence" tab and you'll see a screen similar to Figure 10-9.

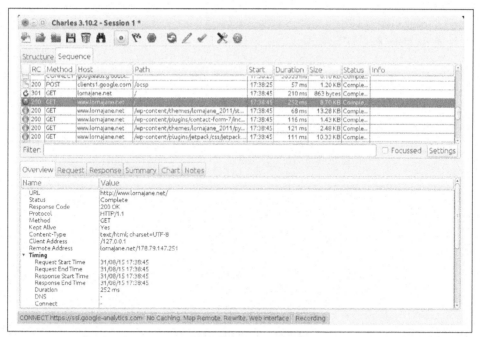

Figure 10-9. Charles showing some web requests in detail

The top part of the pane is a list of requests that came through the proxy, and when you select one of these, the detail shows in the bottom pane. This area has tabs upon tabs, making all kinds of information available for inspection. There are the headers and body of the request and response, including format-aware information on the response so if you receive JSON, XML, or HTML for example, it will be helpfully decoded and displayed as appropriate.

If there's a particular response that allows you to observe a bug, you might like to *repeat* it; Charles makes this much easier than having to click around the same loop again to replicate the bug. Simply locate the request you want in the top pane, and right-click on it to see "Repeat" in the context menu. This is really helpful for debugging, especially as you can export and import sessions from Charles, so you can pass this information around between team members. If one developer is able to replicate the bug but not necessarily fix it at that moment, the session can be saved and attached to the ticket in the issue tracker for another developer to pick up at a later date. Very efficient!

Probably the nicest feature of Charles is its ability to show you SSL (Secure Socket Layer, or https) traffic without needing the private key from the server (which Wireshark requires). SSL is, by its very nature, not something than can be observed from the outside, so usually the result is something like the image in Figure 10-10.

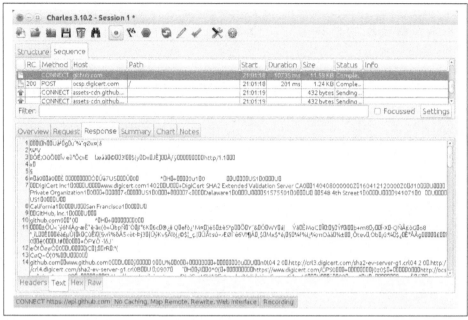

Figure 10-10. Charles showing https traffic without decrypting

Charles allows you to inspect SSL by performing a classic "man in the middle" attack. The traffic between Charles and the remote site is encrypted using the correct certificate as normal, but the traffic between Charles and your browser or other client is only signed by Charles. This means that in order to use this feature in Charles you will need to actively enable Charles' SSL certificates (look in the "SSL" tab on the proxy settings screen) and then accept the Charles CA on the device or client that is sending the SSL traffic.

Charles offers the ability to throttle all traffic that passes through it. Throttling traffic allows you to simulate a selection of real-world network speeds, including 3G for a mobile phone. This is a key part of the development process, especially if your application and server are on a fast corporate network; the real world can look quite different! I will never forget testing games on phones in an underground car park to find out what happened when there was no reception—very glad that nowadays I can just push that traffic through Charles to test these things.

There are two similar features for rewriting requests that I use when passing traffic through Charles. The first is simply called "Rewrite"—it makes it possible to change headers or bodies of requests or responses, restrict them to specific sites, and use regexes to match and change specific elements. This can be handy for all kinds of reasons: trying out a new remote service, or testing whether a change of headers fixes a particular problem. I also use the "Map Remote" feature, which is really helpful when requests arrive at Charles needing a consistent change to their URL. This is perhaps most useful for hardcoded image URLs, but I also use it when using Charles to route a mobile app to a local version of an API rather than the official one.

Using Charles to proxy traffic from a mobile device, whether to rewrite or just to inspect it, is a very useful feature. To set it up:

- Configure the device networking to be on the same network as Charles, and set the proxy to be the IP address of the machine running Charles and the port number it is running on (the default is 8888).
- Either use an app on your device or the mobile browser
- When you first set this up, Charles needs you to confirm that you want to allow this device to proxy through your machine. This is good; it means you're not running an open proxy on your laptop
- The traffic is visible in Charles.

While I mostly use Charles for development purposes, particularly for testing issues on mobile apps where I want to diagnose an issue but I don't want to rebuild the app itself, it's also pretty interesting just to set up the proxy on your device, use your favorite apps, and look at the traffic that they send.

Proxying PHP Applications

Some of these tools, such as Charles, require you to redirect your web traffic through them. We've seen simple examples of how to use a web browser with an add-on or a mobile device to proxy, but what about a PHP application running on your local machine or a development virtual machine? When we work with APIs often the requests are actually made by PHP itself rather than by a client, so an alternative approach is needed.

One option is simply to change the endpoint that we're calling to such that it points to Charles, and then rewrite the request when it arrives at Charles so that it goes on to the right place. That will work, but it's rather a blunt instrument. Instead, we can configure PHP to use proxy settings when making requests.

Proxy Settings for Guzzle

The Guzzle library, which has been used in examples throughout this book, observes a standard environment variable called HTTP_PROXY (frustratingly, command-line cURL respects the same environment variable but in lowercase). You can set the environment variable in your web server config; for example, I'm using Apache and want to proxy through Charles on my host machine which the guest sees as 10.0.2.2, so I add the following line to my vhost configuration:

```
SetEnv HTTP_PROXY http://10.0.2.2:8888
```

Remember to restart Apache after adding this to the vhost configuration, and you should start to see that requests made by Guzzle are proxied through Charles.

Proxy Settings for HTTP Stream Handling

PHP's stream handling doesn't observe the standard environment variable, but it is easy to add proxy settings to the stream context used. In the situation where there is already an $options variable with some settings in it, and again the code should proxy via Charles on 10.0.2.2, the following should be added:

```
$options['http']['proxy'] = "tcp://10.0.2.2:8888";
$streamContext = stream_context_create($options);
```

Pass in this context to the stream and it will proxy requests through the address you specify. Notice that the proxy address starts with tcp:// rather than http://, a common (and very tempting) mistake.

Finding the Tool for the Job

This chapter covered a selection of tools for varying tasks, although there is some overlap, for example, in tools you can use to inspect traffic (in that particular case I usually run Wireshark immediately and then move on to Charles for more detailed debugging, as it's more HTTP-aware but requires me to proxy my traffic through it). I strongly recommend you take the time to play with and get to know these tools and any additional or alternative ones you come across. Knowing what tools are available and how they can help you means being able to rescue yourself and your projects from a tight spot if you need to. I hope you won't ever need to play "hero" when something goes wrong but if you do, you'll be glad you invested some time in stocking your toolbox.

CHAPTER 11

Maintainable Web Services

When we build APIs, perhaps even more than web frontends, these projects should be able to live and thrive over a long period of time. With that in mind, it is prudent to build services that are intended to last and that give consideration to how they can be extended, maintained, and debugged if the need should arise. In Chapter 10 we saw a selection of great external tools that will accompany the work we do with APIs, but what about the APIs themselves? This chapter deals with the very important work of how to structure your API with great error handling and diagnostic output to make a project that can be picked up and maintained for as long as it is needed.

Sample API Application

This chapter is all about how to debug APIs and to do that, we'll use an absolutely trivially simple API as our example. The idea is to show a very simple use case with a minimal amount of code to illustrate the techniques that can be scaled up and applied to your real-world applications.

The example API uses the Slim (*http://www.slimframework.com*) microframework as a lightweight way of quickly starting up a new application. This API is very simple and only has a handful of endpoints:

- /, the root, just returns a list of endpoints.
- /list can be accessed via GET in which case it returns a list of items, or via POST in which case it adds the supplied item to the list.

The code for this is in Example 11-1 and you'll find the formatter just a little further along in Example 11-2. The only initial dependency is the Slim framework, so *composer.json* looks like this:

```
    {
        "require": {
            "slim/slim": "^3.0"
        }
    }
```

Example 11-1. Example API code

```php
<?php

require "../vendor/autoload.php";
require "Formatter.php";

$app = new \Slim\App();

$container = $app->getContainer();
$container['formatter'] = function ($c) {
    return new Formatter($c->get('request'));
};

$app->get(
    '/',
    function ($request, $response) {
        $data = ["home" => "/", "list" => "/list"];
        $response = $this->formatter->render($response, $data);
        return $response;
    }
);

$app->get(
    "/list",
    function ($request, $response) {
        // fetch items
        $items = [];
        $fp = fopen('../items.csv', 'r');
        while(false !== ($data = fgetcsv($fp))) {
            $items[] = current($data);
        }

        $data = ["items" => $items, "count" => count($items)];
        $response = $this->formatter->render($response, $data);
        return $response;
    }
);

$app->post(
    "/list",
    function($request, $response) {
        $data = $request->getParsedBody();

        if(isset($data) && isset($data['item']) && !empty($data['item'])) {
            $this->logger->addInfo("Adding data item: " . $data['item']);
```

```
        // save item
        $fp = fopen('../items.csv', 'a');
        fputcsv($fp, [$data['item']]);

        $response = $response
            ->withStatus(201)
            ->withHeader("Location", "/list");

        $response = $this->formatter->render($response);
        return $response;
    }

    // if we got this far, something went really wrong
    throw new UnexpectedValueException("Item could not be parsed");
    }
);

$app->run();
```

This very simple example forms the basis upon which we'll add some particular features that will make an API maintainable and easy to work with in development and for a long and happy maintenance window.

Consistent Output Formats

This is the golden rule: *always* respond in the format that the client was expecting. This means that it is never acceptable to return an HTML error message when the client expected JSON—but beware that many of the frameworks will do exactly this by default when an error occurs! If your system does return HTML messages when things go wrong, that is a bug and needs fixing. If an unexpected format is sent, the client will not be unable to understand the response and any error information contained in it.

One of the side effects of using the Slim framework is that it offers the getParsed Body() method on the Request object, which essentially means that our API already supports multiple input formats. This method reads the Content-Type header of the incoming request, and parses the body data accordingly. As a result, if you POST data from a form, or send JSON data with an appropriate Content-Type header, then Slim will parse that accordingly.

The example code handles multiple output formats by using an output renderer, which is the Formatter class added to the container and then used in each endpoint. The code for the Formatter class is in Example 11-2, and it takes care of getting the right output format (the HTML version is quite basic in an attempt to keep the code samples shorter) and the right headers in accordance with the Accept header that was received.

Example 11-2. The Formatter class is used as an output renderer, ensuring data is returned in a correct and consistent format

```php
<?php

class Formatter
{
    protected $request;

    public function __construct($request) {
        $this->request = $request;
    }

    public function render($response, $data = [])
    {
        if ($data) {
            $format = $this->getFormatFromAcceptHeader();

            switch ($format) {
                case 'html':
                    $body = $response->getBody();
                    // very ugly output but you get the idea
                    $body = $response->getBody();
                    $body->write(var_export($data, true));
                    break;

                case 'json':
                default:
                    $body = $response->getBody();
                    $body->write(json_encode($data));
                    $response = $response
                        ->withHeader("Content-Type", "application/json");
            }
        }
        return $response;
    }

    protected function getFormatFromAcceptHeader() {
        $accept = explode(
            ',',
            $this->request->getHeaderLine("Accept")
        );

        // we prefer JSON
        $format = 'json';

        // we also support HTML
        if (in_array("text/html", $accept)
            || in_array("application/xhtml+xml", $accept)) {
            $format = 'html';
        }
```

```
            return $format;
    }
}
```

There's a method here that does basic `Accept` header parsing (for a more comprehensive approach revisit the content negotiation section in Chapter 3) so we need to supply the `$request` object in order to make that information available. Once the correct format has been identified, the supplied data array is converted and set on the `$response` object along with appropriate headers.

There are a few Slim-specific features in the code shown here that might look different in another framework or without a framework at all, so it's worth identifying those and giving the "vanilla" PHP equivalents in case you need them. All of these have been seen in examples throughout the rest of the book.

- `$response->withStatus()` in Slim simply sets the status code, so use `http_response_code()` in PHP.

- Each call to `$response->withHeader()` could be replaced in a PHP application with a call to `header()`, in which case the two arguments are put into one string and separated by a colon, e.g., `Content-Type: application/json`.

- The Slim function `$request->getParsedBody()` is a very neat feature that wraps up a read from `php://input`, checks the incoming `Content-Type` header, and in this case identifies JSON and does a `json_decode()` accordingly

Each framework will have its own way of doing the same things, but you'll find that the modern frameworks all use a very similar approach since the shape of the request and response objects is related to the standards laid out in PSR-7 (*http://www.php-fig.org/psr/psr-7*), which covers HTTP Messaging.

With this simple sample app (and some data already in the low-tech storage solution *items.csv*) it is possible to look at ways that debugging techniques can be used with an API.

Debug Output as a Tool

Every PHP developer will have used `print_r()` or `var_dump()` at some point to return some additional information to the client during the course of the server processing a request. This technique is quick, easy, approachable, and can often be all that is needed to spot a typo or missing value.

When working with APIs, this can still sometimes be useful, but it does carry health warnings! If standard debug output is included with a response, and the client is expecting valid JSON, XML, or some other format, then your client will not be able to parse the response. Instead, try making the call from another tool such as the ones we saw in Chapter 10.

A great example would be to add a `var_dump()` call to the `/list` endpoint of the API, so that the route now looks like this:

```
$app->get(
    "/list",
    function ($request, $response) {
        // fetch items
        $items = [];
        $fp = fopen('../items.csv', 'r');
        while(false !== ($data = fgetcsv($fp))) {
            $items[] = current($data);
        }
        var_dump($items);
        exit;
    }
);
```

 When adding code that dumps output, it's simplest to follow it with `exit()` so that no other code will execute after that point and possibly obscure the behavior that you were trying to observe.

I can inspect this in any one of a number of ways:

- Use cURL, HTTPie, Postman, or any similar tools to make the API call that I want to debug. The preceding example can be seen in Example 11-3.

- If it's easy to replicate from a client that can't display the response, use Wireshark, Charles, or mitmproxy to inspect the response; just ignore the client errors since we know we're sending back invalid JSON. Figure 11-1 shows the previous example inspected via Charles.

Example 11-3. Use cURL to inspect debug output added to an API call

```
$ curl -v http://localhost:8080/list
* Hostname was NOT found in DNS cache
*    Trying 127.0.0.1...
* Connected to localhost (127.0.0.1) port 8080 (#0)
> GET /list HTTP/1.1
> User-Agent: curl/7.38.0
> Host: localhost:8080
> Accept: */*
>
< HTTP/1.1 200 OK
< Host: localhost:8080
```

```
< Connection: close
< X-Powered-By: PHP/5.6.4-4ubuntu6
< Content-type: text/html; charset=UTF-8
<
array(4) {
  [0]=>
  string(5) "bread"
  [1]=>
  string(4) "eggs"
  [2]=>
  string(4) "milk"
  [3]=>
  string(6) "apples"
}
* Closing connection 0
```

Figure 11-1. Using Charles to inspect debug output from an API

If it's an AJAX call that is failing, your browser tools should allow you to copy the failing request as a cURL request. Then it's easy to repeat, or to share with your coworkers to enable debugging.

Don't be afraid to use the fast-and-dirty approach to debug APIs exactly as you might take a first look at any other PHP problem. It's a little harder to see when the output doesn't just appear in the browser, but this section illustrated how to take the extra step to make the output visible.

Effective Logging Techniques

When it is important to continue returning clean responses, more information can be acquired from an API, as it processes requests, by adding logging. This just means that, rather than sending debug information along with the output, it is sent somewhere else to be inspected (usually to a file on the server).

By default, PHP will write errors to the location specified in the configuration directive error_log in *php.ini*. If this is left empty, then PHP defaults to writing to Apache's error log (or stderr, if you're not using Apache). It is possible to write other information to this log, as well as the errors generated by PHP itself, using the error_log() function:

```php
<?php

error_log("this is an error!");
```

Perhaps this looks like a rather oversimplified example, but at its most basic level this is all that is needed to add logging. When I look in the Apache error log on the server (the exact file location varies between platforms), I see this:

```
[Wed Dec 26 14:49:36 2015] [error] [client 127.0.0.1] this is an error!,
referer: http://localhost:8080/
[Wed Dec 26 14:49:36 2015] [error] [client 127.0.0.1] File does not
exist: /var/www/favicon.ico
```

A couple of errors can be seen in the previous output. The first was sent by the code sample, which deliberately wrote a message to the error log, and the other is what happened when my browser requested a favicon, but none existed. Using this approach, error_log() calls can be added into a project to help debug a particular issue. The output from the error log can then be checked to discover the additional information needed, rather than sending the additional error information back to the client.

Logging is a powerful technique; there are many more tricks available to make it even more effective. Log messages can be directed to a specific file, for example, rather than to the generic error log. To do this, use the `error_log()` function but with some additional arguments. The first argument is the message, as before, the second argument is where to send the message (3 means "to a file"; for more detail see PHP's error log documentation (*http://bit.ly/php-error-log*)), and the final argument is the filename to use:

```php
<?php

error_log("all gone wrong", 3, "log.txt");
```

The file should be writeable by the user that the web server represents, and then the error message will appear in the file (beware: it doesn't add a new line after each message). Specifying a file means that all the debug information can be kept in one place and will be easy to follow. The file could be truncated between test runs to make it even clearer exactly what happened in any given scenario.

There are lots of excellent libraries around to make logging easier, and if you're using a framework, it will probably offer some great logging functionality. There are some great features in dedicated logging tools or modules that will help keep track of what's happening in your application without resorting to a `var_dump()` call in the middle of your JSON output. When selecting a logging solution, look out for:

Multiple storage options
> Many logging libraries support more ways to store log entries than just email or files. Usually it's possible to log in to many different kinds of databases, use various file formats, and set other options. Depending on how you want to use the data, this can be very useful indeed.

Configurable logging levels
> Logging libraries usually allow you to state the level of error that is being logged; this is comparable to the PHP approach of having ERROR, WARN, NOTICE, and so on. The application allows you to set what level of logging should be performed. This means you can change the logging levels on a lower-traffic test platform when you want to see more detail, or increase them temporarily to see more detail during a particular set of operations. As a result, the log files don't become too huge when things are going well, but more detail can be obtained when required.

Standards compliant
> There is a PHP standard interface for logging tools called PSR-3. Choosing a logging tool that complies with this means that you can change between logging tools in the future if you should wish to.

Error Logging in PHP Applications with Monolog

One very good and widely used tool for logging in PHP is Monolog (*https://github.com/Seldaek/monolog*). This satisfies all of the key points just listed and as a bonus you'll find that many PHP frameworks either include it by default or offer their own wrappers for it.

To add Monolog to our existing example, the first step is to add it to *composer.json*, which now looks like this:

```
{
    "require": {
        "slim/slim": "^3.0",
        "monolog/monolog": "^1.17"
    }
}
```

Once the dependencies are in place, a logger can be created. Monolog supports a brilliant and extensive selection of handlers including writing to a file, to email, to databases, to remote services, to firebug, and the list goes on. In this example the logger simply writes to a file called *app.log*, but having many possibilities as well as the option to combine some or all of the above at different logging levels is very useful especially as to change what we log and how is purely done here in the setup and then takes effect throughout our application.

Since the API example uses the Slim framework, it comes with a dependency injection container, so we create our logger and put it into the container, so we can use it anywhere in the application. The code for this goes right at the top of the example and is laid out in Example 11-4.

Example 11-4. Construct the logger and store it in the dependency injection container

```php
<?php

require "../vendor/autoload.php";

$app = new \Slim\App();

// create the logger, add to DI container
$container = $app->getContainer();
$container['logger'] = function($c) {
    $logger = new \Monolog\Logger('my_logger');
    $file_handler = new \Monolog\Handler\StreamHandler("../app.log");
    $logger->pushHandler($file_handler);
    return $logger;
};
```

Now that the logger is in place, it can be used to record error or debug messages at the appropriate error level. The key thing about error levels is that there can be many log entries added to the code, and we can configure our applications to show all levels on a development platform, but only log the really big things on a production platform...unless things go wrong, in which case we can easily reconfigure to get more information.

In this example, let's add some logging to the POST endpoint to record when we receive a new list item. The updated route code is now in Example 11-5. It simply accesses the stored logger property from earlier (Slim has some magic that makes items in its dependency injection container available as properties) and calls the Monolog function addInfo() upon it, passing in the message we'd like to render.

Example 11-5. Using Monolog in our existing code

```
$app->post(
    "/list",
    function($request, $response) {
        $data = $request->getParsedBody();

        if(isset($data) && isset($data->item) && !empty($data->item)) {
            $this->logger->addInfo("Adding data item: " . $data->item);
            // save item
            $fp = fopen('../items.csv', 'a');
            fputcsv($fp, [$data->item]);

            $response = $response
                ->withStatus(201)
                ->withHeader("Location", "/list");

            $response = $this->formatter->render($response);
            return $response;
        }
    }
);
```

With the logger in place, if I POST to the endpoint to create a new list item, I get a log entry that looks something like this:

```
[2015-09-05 16:41:27] my_logger.INFO: Adding data item: cheese [] []
```

It is good practice to have logging in place for all our applications, but for APIs where the problems can be a few layers down from the interface that humans see, it's a must-have. Monolog is only one choice, but it's an excellent one and it allows us to configure much more on an application level than the PHP error_log() function.

Error Handling with PHP Exceptions

PHP offers really excellent error handling with its Exception (*http://bit.ly/php-exception*) class. This works similarly to exceptions in other object-oriented languages: you can throw an exception in your code, and it will then "bubble" up the stack by swiftly returning from each level of function call until it lands in either a `catch()` block or an exception handler.

While there are many great resources on PHP error handling around, there's one particular feature in PHP that I make extensive use of, and that's the ability to set a top-level exception handler. Whether that's setting the error-handling feature in a framework (as will be seen in a Slim example momentarily) or using the standard `set_exception_handler()`, this ability to handle errors in the same way throughout the application is very helpful in APIs, in particular where a common output handler is often used.

When something goes wrong in an application, we throw an exception. While it's possible to use a generic `Exception` class in PHP, it's also very easy to extend that class and include the new class (often with no additional functionality) in your own code base. The big advantage of taking this approach is that you can then distinguish between the exception type you were expecting and something completely unexpected happening.

 PHP also includes a good selection of built-in exceptions you can use; see the manual (*http://bit.ly/php-exceptions*) for a list.

Exceptions always include a descriptive error message, but it's important to consider where this error message will be seen. This chapter already covered some techniques for logging information, and as a general rule of thumb it is useful to include enough information to understand what went wrong in the exception; any information that should not be displayed to a user or other consumer can instead be logged.

A simple example of throwing an exception can be seen at the very end of Example 11-6 where in the event that we don't get valid data, we use the exception handler to return that. The exception here is an `UnexpectedValueException`, which is one of PHP's built-in exception types.

Example 11-6. Exception is thrown if the expected data doesn't arrive

```
$app->post(
    "/list",
    function($request, $response) {
        $data = $request->getParsedBody();

        if(isset($data) && isset($data->item) && !empty($data->item)) {
            $this->logger->addInfo("Adding data item: " . $data->item);
            // save item
```

```
        $fp = fopen('../items.csv', 'a');
        fputcsv($fp, [$data->item]);

        $response = $response
            ->withStatus(201)
            ->withHeader("Location", "/list");

        $response = $this->formatter->render($response);
        return $response;
    }

    // if we got this far, something went really wrong
    throw new UnexpectedValueException("Item could not be parsed");
    }
);
```

In addition to the message, an exception can also have a code. Since HTTP has status codes, it can be useful to supply the code as well as the message in the exception, since in this case the exception handler will be formatting the error output.

So how can we craft an exception handler that will parse this Exception object and return the response that the API consumer can understand? The key things here are to be consistent, and to always return in the format (e.g., JSON, XML) that the client is expecting, even through we're returning unexpected content.

The example we've just reviewed would want an exception handler to catch any Exceptions that haven't been dealt with in any other way. Mine looks something like the example in Example 11-7. It takes the exception, sets the given status code or a generic 400 if it's missing, and returns an error message in the body (in the Slim framework, you need to unset the $container[errorHandler] to be able to add your own standard PHP exception handler; other frameworks will also have their own ways of doing things).

Example 11-7. Exception handler from the sample project

```
set_exception_handler(function ($exception) {
    if($exception->getCode()) {
        http_response_code($exception->getCode());
    } else {
        http_response_code(400);
    }

    header("Content-Type: application/json");
    echo json_encode(["message" => $exception->getMessage()]);
});
```

With the added Exception from Example 11-6, my output looks like this when I make a POST request with no data:

```
$ curl -v -X POST -H "Content-Type: application/json" http://localhost:8080/list
* Hostname was NOT found in DNS cache
*   Trying 127.0.0.1...
* Connected to localhost (127.0.0.1) port 8080 (#0)
> POST /list HTTP/1.1
> User-Agent: curl/7.38.0
> Host: localhost:8080
> Accept: */*
> Content-Type: application/json
>
< HTTP/1.1 400 Bad Request
< Host: localhost:8080
< Connection: close
< X-Powered-By: PHP/5.6.4-4ubuntu6
< Content-Type: application/json
<
* Closing connection 0
{"message":"Item could not be parsed"}
```

The status code and headers are important, but this also includes a readable message so even if we were consuming it without the -v switch, we'd see something. For example, if I just pass the body output through jq, I'd see this:

```
$ curl -s -X POST -H "Content-Type: application/json" http://localhost:8080/
list | jq "."
{
    "message": "Item could not be parsed"
}
```

In PHP 5, the exception handler will catch any uncaught object extending Exception, regardless of whether it came from your code, from a library, or from PHP itself. In PHP 7, the exception handler will catch anything that is both uncaught and that implements the new Throwable interface. This will probably behave as you expect in that it will still catch your Exception objects as before, but it will also catch any uncaught Error objects. You may see changes to when the exception handler is fired after you upgrade your existing applications, and it's worth bearing in mind that this could mean catching objects whose messages you might not automatically want to expose to the outside world.

Using this exception handler pattern is a great way to ensure consistency of output so that your error messages are always delivered in a predictable way and in the expected format so that a client can understand them.

With error handling in place, it's important to have test coverage of those failure cases as well as the successful ones; you can read more about testing tools in "Automated Testing Tools" on page 151 along with other key delivery tools for APIs. At this point, we have covered the tools needed to add diagnostic, logging, and error-handling features to an API—we will discuss some of the finer points of API design in the following chapters.

CHAPTER 12

Making Service Design Decisions

This is the million-dollar question: what kind of a service do I need for my next project? REST is cool, but RPC is familiar. JSON is lighter, but the client already works with XML. The API will be used by mobile consumers, or web consumers, or a reporting engine, or all of these.

There's rarely a clear-cut "one true way" when picking the best solution for a given API, but there are some key elements that can influence how to choose a solution that will be a good fit. API design is mostly engineering with a generous dash of common sense also required.

The big questions you need to ask at each step are these:

1. Who will be using this API?

2. What are they trying to achieve?

3. Which technologies do they use?

There are some key points that are important to consider when planning an API that will help us answer these questions and deliver an effective API.

Consider the users' needs

The API will be needed and utilized by users, not developers. Start out with a comprehensive set of user stories about how users intend to use the API, the kind of people that will be using it, and the technologies they are likely to want to use. Beginning from the point of view of what a user wants to achieve, rather than a developer's preferred toolchain, is more likely to give a good API outcome.

Eat your own dogfood

The term "dogfood" is a bit of a strange one but it means to incorporate the tools you make and publish into your own workflows where you can. This means not building an application with its own business logic and a separate API for outsiders to use, but instead building an API that is used both internally and externally. If you don't need to make use of the API, it's a good idea to at least build a sample application and think about the challenges a user might encounter.

Keep it simple

Don't plan a huge API and publish the whole thing at once. Decide which of your user stories constitute the MVP (Minimum Viable Product) for your consumers, and start with that. In Chapter 14 we'll cover all the other various parts of delivering the API besides just the API itself. By starting small, it's a great chance for a development team to make sure that the documentation, deployment, testing, and all the other associated tools are also in place and working well.

Service Type Decisions

The first decision to make when designing any API is one that can't be changed: decide what kind of a service you will offer. This depends on a combination of the audience and the features that will be offered.

If the service mostly deals with creating, fetching, and manipulating data, then a RESTful service should definitely be a candidate in your design decision. In Chapter 8 we discussed how everything in a RESTful service is either a collection or a resource, and if the service you have in mind mostly deals with *things* or groups of *things* then REST is going to be a great fit. It's increasingly widely used and there are some excellent resources available specifically about designing RESTful services, independent of which language you implement it in (but PHP is a great choice).

For an API that *does* actions rather than working with *things*, an RPC service might be a more logical choice to make. RPC services are a very familiar paradigm for developers of all kinds and so they can offer a shallower learning curve to people integrating with external APIs for the first time. It might be useful to look at some of the existing services cited in Chapter 7 to get an idea of whether those feel like the kind of thing you are aiming for.

Another consideration is how easy your chosen type of service will be to build, deliver, and maintain with consideration to the technology stack and abilities of the consumers; some technology communities are much more familiar with SOAP for example, and would prefer a service with a WSDL that will bolt in nicely to their existing platform. Whereas a mobile developer would probably prefer something more lightweight such as a RESTful JSON API.

How to Present API Data

A SOAP service will always use XML, but for RESTful or RPC services, the data format that fits best can be chosen. The most common options are JSON and XML, but there are also services that handle incoming form-encoded data formats, outgoing HTML formats, serialized PHP formats, YAML, and even plain text.

We saw in Chapter 6 some examples of XML being used with an RPC service, and SOAP is XML underneath. However, XML has plenty more applications than just SOAP, and can be used as the data format (or *a* data format) in any one of a number of different styles of service. XML allows us to mark up elements with child elements, character data, and also attributes, but produces quite a large data size in return. Therefore, XML would do well when the bandwidth used for the transfers isn't slow or expensive, and the devices consuming the data have enough memory and processing power to handle and parse the data.

JSON is great for JavaScript applications, but they're not the only target market for this format. The majority of scripting languages have built-in support for JSON and will be able to serve and consume this format easily. JSON is also a great choice for mobile applications, where the smaller overall data size and simplicity of parsing the format are very useful for less powerful devices on potentially slow, patchy, or expensive connections.

HTML as a data format is an idea that isn't found in many textbooks, but certainly shows up in the real world on a regular basis. In its simplest form, we might return HTML in response to an AJAX request from a webpage, perhaps showing some new content in HTML on the page (something that you may already feature in your applications). It doesn't take a huge leap of faith from this to providing HTML as an optional output format for an API, if only for reading data. An example of this is found in the RESTful Joind.in API, where HTML is offered as an output format; if you request *http://api.joind.in* from your browser, the API reads your Accept headers and returns the data as HTML, with the hypermedia presented as clickable hyperlinks. This serves as excellent documentation for your service.

Accepting incoming requests from a web form, or in that format, can also be very web-friendly if the users of the API are mostly web developers and it is likely to be used mostly with or from a web page. This is a step away from the pure idea of exchanging data between machines, but can be a valuable option depending on the audience of the API.

If the user stories show that different consumers will want different data formats, then the API will need to return *multiple formats* such as XML, JSON, and perhaps HTML as well. This approach has major advantages because every consumer of your service will be able to ask for the data in the format that is right for their scenario, using content negotiation via HTTP headers to indicate what the right format is. An application that takes care to make use of common templates or output handlers for each data format, used by every response sent, will be able to consistently return data in multiple formats.

Hypermedia for Easy API Navigation

The links to resources and related data in an API are called *hypermedia* and are an excellent feature to include. In a RESTful service particularly, every resource is identified by its URI and so this data can be given as part of the response data. In this way, consuming clients can follow links, rather like a user clicking links on the Web, instead of assembling the next URL from the instructions and concatenating ID fields into it. Hypermedia makes the whole experience smoother and easier for consumers by offering the ability to find their way around easily. For example, using the previous data set, the following actions are available:

1. Look at this resource (*http://api.joind.in/v2.1/talks/7660*), and then visit the `comments_uri` to see the comments made on this talk.

2. See more information about the event this talk belongs to by visiting the `event_uri` (*http://api.joind.in/v2.1/events/1056*).

3. From there, follow another piece of hypermedia in the `talks_uri` field to see a list of other talks at the event (*http://api.joind.in/v2.1/events/1056/talks*).

Nested Data or Many Round Trips

Another consideration when designing and working with RESTful APIs is whether or not it is useful to send additional nested data with the response to avoid a consumer having to make too many "round trips," or requests and responses, to get the rest of the information desired. While GitHub and Joind.in both offer user information at their own locations, they also include some nested data in the responses shown here, which the consumer is likely to need.

On the other hand, sometimes too much information can lead to unnecessarily large amounts of data to transfer, and different APIs handle this in different ways. One common pattern is that, by default, a subset of the information is returned, but functionality to retrieve more information is also offered—this is what the Joind.in `verbose_uri` offers. Alternatively, the extra information may be made available as a separate resource, such as offering `/article/42` as the data about a blog post, but excluding the (potentially large) body of the post, which can then be found at `/article/42/body`. Either approach shows consideration to the consumer, but which one is the right fit will depend on any particular scenario.

Some of the common API formats have provisions for controlling how much detail is returned when they request data, or which related data should be included with the response. Let's look more at some of those data formats.

Data Formats and Media Types

A single web service can offer a selection of data types, and it's very common to offer multiple types. Often, these will be JSON or XML, but there can be others; for example, Joind.in will respond to GET requests with an HTML data type if the Accept header requests it. The format decision will be made on the server, usually on the basis of the Accept header (you can read more about content negotiation in "Headers for Content Negotiation" on page 30).

Some services will allow a content indicator to be present in the URL itself, but this mixes up the identification of the resource with information about the representation desired. In general, the Accept header is the "right" way to indicate the preferred format, while supporting an additional URL parameter may lower the barrier of entry, depending on your consumers.

So you might offer two ways of requesting JSON data:

- By setting the Accept header to "application/json"—this would be the preferred method.

- Not all clients (or all developers) are capable of setting custom headers, so you might also allow the appending of ?format=json or the equivalent to a request.

 Don't be tempted to add a .json suffix to your URL to allow clients to request JSON, especially in a RESTful service. The URI should point to a resource without specific format information, and then headers or additional parameters can be used to give extra information to the server about how we'd like that response served.

There are some very good prescribed data formats that you might like to consider for your applications. Beyond touching on JSON-RPC and XML-RPC earlier in the book, two other good candidates to consider are HAL and JSON-API. They do all differ in some ways, but each of them aims to make a scalable and consistent API for users by describing how data and hypermedia can be presented. The following sections have some examples of these formats to give you an idea of what to expect.

HAL (Hypertext Application Language) is a standard that aims to make it easy to traverse an API that you haven't seen before and find your way around. It can be used with both XML and JSON and aims to describe hypermedia in a useful and importantly a consistent way across APIs.

The best features of HAL are the _links collections that it uses to bring hypermedia into a known location and a known format. The _links collections are used both at the top level of a response to include some metadata such as pagination, and also within representations to give related links to the item. The _links collection has a named key that indicates what this link is, and then an array containing at least an href value, although other information can also be included.

The result looks something like Example 12-1, which uses the same talk resource as mentioned in the hypermedia section earlier.

Example 12-1. Adding HAL to the joind.in API talk resource

```
{
  "_links": {
    "self": "http://api.joind.in/v2.1/talks/7660?start=0&resultsperpage=20"
  },
  "talks": [
    {
      "_links": {
        "self": "http://api.joind.in/v2.1/talks/7660",
        "verbose_self": "http://api.joind.in/v2.1/talks/7660?verbose=yes",
        "website_uri": "http://joind.in/talk/view/7660",
        "comments_uri": "http://api.joind.in/v2.1/talks/7660/comments",
        "event_uri": "http://api.joind.in/v2.1/events/1056"
      },
      "talk_title": "Everything You Ever Wanted to Know About Deployment But Were
Afraid to Ask",
      "start_date": "2012-11-08T13:00:00-05:00",
      "average_rating": 5,
      "comment_count": 4
    }
  ]
}
```

HAL also supports embedding related resources within a result set; this is a very common situation to encounter so a standard way of presenting this is very useful. The other big feature in HAL is "curies," which are a way of describing where the documentation can be found for the endpoints in use. Being able to reach documentation related to the request currently being made can be very helpful to users so this is a nice feature to include. You can read more about HAL in the specification (*http:// bit.ly/hal-spec*).

Another format that works very well, especially on RESTful APIs, is JSON-API (*http://jsonapi.org*). As the name suggests, it's for JSON data and much like HAL it sets out some very standard ways of organizing information so that all APIs built along these lines will be familiar. JSON-API describes a series of top-level data elements to use.

- `errors` is a collection of error items
- `meta` gives information not directly related to the data being transferred (JSON-API) can handle either a resource or a collection
- `data` the actual data goes inside this element, always
- `jsonapi` may be used to describe the server implementation
- `links` holds links related to the top level of this endpoint and always includes a `self` link
- `included` can contain related resources, often used to avoid the consumer from having to make multiple calls

It is required to return at least one of `errors`, `meta` and `data`, but beyond that this data format can be adapted to fit your needs. The individual resources each should contain an `id` and a `type`, with its main data in the `attributes` section. Resources can also have their own `links` and `meta` properties.

Using the same talk resource example before, an example of how it might look if returned by a JSON-API service is shown in Example 12-2. As you can see, the two are very similar.

Example 12-2. The talk resource from Joind.in's API formatted in JSON-API

```
{
  "links": {
    "self": "http://api.joind.in/v2.1/talks/7660?start=0&resultsperpage=20"
  },
  "data": [
    {
      "type": "talk",
      "id": 7660,
      "attributes": {
        "talk_title": "Everything You Ever Wanted to Know About Deployment But Were
Afraid to Ask",
        "start_date": "2012-11-08T13:00:00-05:00",
        "average_rating": 5,
        "comment_count": 4
      },
      "links": {
        "self": "http://api.joind.in/v2.1/talks/7660",
        "verbose_self": "http://api.joind.in/v2.1/talks/7660?verbose=yes",
        "website_uri": "http://joind.in/talk/view/7660",
        "comments_uri": "http://api.joind.in/v2.1/talks/7660/comments",
        "event_uri": "http://api.joind.in/v2.1/events/1056"
      }
    }
  ]
}
```

Picking a common format for your API data can be very helpful to allow people to quickly get up to speed and feel "at home." The various API formats are evolving all the time, so it's worth taking a look around at the options and reflecting on your goals for the service you want to publish before you choose. If there's a standard that could fit, always try to use it—standards are always good!

Versioning your API is highly recommended, but of course it isn't obvious that you need it until you want to start work on v2.0! Including a version number in your URL is a matter of taste. It is a very practical way to offer a service while identifying the current version of that service and opening the door to offering new versions of the service in the future. However, there are alternatives, and an elegant alternative is to use *media types*. These are invented content types that specifically describe the structure of the resource that will be returned, and can also include version information, so if the structure of a particular resource changes between versions, that change can be conveyed without a URL change.

Not all APIs will support media types, but they are a good way to version representation structures for users who want to be certain that the representations they receive will never change. GitHub has some media type support (their reference page (*http://developer.github.com/v3/media*) explains the detail very well) that goes beyond the usual `application/json` levels. They support media types specific to GitHub (`application/vnd.github+json`) and also support using the media type to specify the version of representation that should be returned (`application/vnd.github.v3`).

Customizable Experiences

As well as choosing data formats, there are other variables for which the "right" choice to make will differ between the consumers of the API. An easy example is the number of entries you return. Returning all the data is fine…until the application becomes terribly popular, and suddenly the API is returning four thousand records instead of forty! To improve this experience for everyone, APIs often offer pagination of data. As well as giving a way to specify which range of results to return, it is good practice to allow the number of results returned to be customized. A reporting server on a fast network might want all the data, whereas the mobile device with a patchy signal might only want the newest five records.

Another big variable is how much information to return with each request, and this decision usually manifests in two forms. When returning information about a particular item, should *all* the information be returned? And the follow-up question: should any related data be returned also? Including data means we'll sometimes be returning more information than needed, a bit like doing SELECT * FROM… in SQL. But if you omit data, then some consumers will have to make a large number of requests to obtain what they need.

Since we already used GitHub as an example and they do this rather nicely, their gist data format will be a nice example to use. You can see it in Example 12-3.

Example 12-3. Gist data format from GitHub

```
{
  "url": "https://api.github.com/gists/ed972482e08ccddfc993",
  "forks_url": "https://api.github.com/gists/ed972482e08ccddfc993/forks",
  "commits_url": "https://api.github.com/gists/ed972482e08ccddfc993/commits",
  "id": "ed972482e08ccddfc993",
  "git_pull_url": "https://gist.github.com/ed972482e08ccddfc993.git",
  "git_push_url": "https://gist.github.com/ed972482e08ccddfc993.git",
  "html_url": "https://gist.github.com/ed972482e08ccddfc993",
  "files": {
    "text.txt": {
      "filename": "text.txt",
      "type": "text/plain",
      "language": "Text",
      "raw_url": "https://gist.githubusercontent.com/lornajane/
ed972482e08ccddfc993/raw/336516c8e23e55265245bf589ae56aafa9cbbcf2/text.txt",
      "size": 18,
      "truncated": false,
      "content": "Some riveting text"
    }
  },
  "public": true,
  "created_at": "2015-07-23T18:30:11Z",
  "updated_at": "2015-08-29T14:25:41Z",
  "description": "Gist created by API",
  "comments": 0,
  "user": null,
  "comments_url": "https://api.github.com/gists/ed972482e08ccddfc993/comments",
  "owner": {
    "login": "lornajane",
    "id": 172607,
    "avatar_url": "https://avatars.githubusercontent.com/u/172607?v=3",
    "gravatar_id": "",
    "url": "https://api.github.com/users/lornajane",
    "html_url": "https://github.com/lornajane",
    "followers_url": "https://api.github.com/users/lornajane/followers",
    "following_url": "https://api.github.com/users/lornajane/following{/
other_user}",
    "gists_url": "https://api.github.com/users/lornajane/gists{/gist_id}",
    "starred_url": "https://api.github.com/users/lornajane/starred{/owner}{/repo}",
    "subscriptions_url": "https://api.github.com/users/lornajane/subscriptions",
    "organizations_url": "https://api.github.com/users/lornajane/orgs",
    "repos_url": "https://api.github.com/users/lornajane/repos",
    "events_url": "https://api.github.com/users/lornajane/events{/privacy}",
    "received_events_url": "https://api.github.com/users/lornajane/received_events",
    "type": "User",
    "site_admin": false
```

```
    },
    "forks": [

    ],
    "history": [
      {
        "user": {
          "login": "lornajane",
          "id": 172607,
          "avatar_url": "https://avatars.githubusercontent.com/u/172607?v=3",
          "gravatar_id": "",
          "url": "https://api.github.com/users/lornajane",
          "html_url": "https://github.com/lornajane",
          "followers_url": "https://api.github.com/users/lornajane/followers",
          "following_url": "https://api.github.com/users/lornajane/
          following{/other_user}",
          "gists_url": "https://api.github.com/users/lornajane/gists{/gist_id}",
          "starred_url": "https://api.github.com/users/lornajane/
          starred{/owner}{/repo}",
          "subscriptions_url": "https://api.github.com/users/lornajane/subscriptions",
          "organizations_url": "https://api.github.com/users/lornajane/orgs",
          "repos_url": "https://api.github.com/users/lornajane/repos",
          "events_url": "https://api.github.com/users/lornajane/events{/privacy}",
          "received_events_url": "https://api.github.com/users/lornajane/
received_events",
          "type": "User",
          "site_admin": false
        },
        "version": "a06b78d732925104c79256e58e84f74af8c579f2",
        "committed_at": "2015-07-23T18:30:11Z",
        "change_status": {
          "total": 1,
          "additions": 1,
          "deletions": 0
        },
        "url": "https://api.github.com/gists/ed972482e08ccddfc993/
a06b78d732925104c79256e58e84f74af8c579f2"
      }
    ]
}
```

This example is a nice combination of nested and linked data. It's quite long, but it also means that consumers don't need to make a lot of requests to get the data they are likely to want. For example, the owner information is included and has most of the data you get from the user URL itself, but the comments aren't nested and instead we get a count and a link to them.

Some APIs allow the user to specify which nested items should be included, or which fields should be returned, which can be handy if, for example, one of the fields is very large. A great example of this is JSON-API, which supports both of these via its `include` and `fields` parameters.

For each service that is built, an important part of the design process is to make decisions about some of these elements. Whatever you decide for your own applications, make sure that you are consistent across your API and that if you do add optional ways of customizing output, that these are well documented.

Pick Your Defaults

It's important to offer users some choice, but also to offer a simpler path so that people can jump straight in and use your API without having to set up too many options. Every customizable option should have a default value that is returned if no preference is stated. Are you missing the Accept header? Send JSON. You don't have any pagination settings? Send the first 25 results. This approach allows people to get the best of the API very quickly and easily, and they can delve deeper to change the defaults if their requirements don't fit well with the defaults chosen.

Consider whether or not you will comply with all requests, though; if a consumer requests 1,000 results that might be expensive for your API to generate, you may still only send the first 200 (or whatever makes sense for your system). Similarly, some APIs will benefit from having rate limits. This means that each client can only make a certain number of requests in a given time period. Many APIs allow a very limited number of requests for unregistered users, and may allow differing levels of access to different customers, particularly for paid-for apps. Rate limiting is a way of making sure that you guarantee an expected level of service to all users by managing the load on your servers and allowing different users to have a level of access that suits them.

This philosophy of making things easy and useful to users, with minimal effort on their part, makes the barrier to entry much lower for your application and makes the experience of using a new API one of tolerance and welcome.

CHAPTER 13

Building a Robust Service

A robust service is one that feels secure and reliable to its users. Something that behaves unpredictably, sometimes gives incorrect results, and occasionally doesn't respond at all, is not what a consumer wants to integrate into her own applications. This chapter will look at what makes a robust service, and some techniques for making services as reliable and useful as they can be, both when things are going well and when they are not.

The best services exhibit consistent, predictable behaviors. This approach of having as much "sameness" as possible works well for consumers, who start to feel at home. As they use the service, they become familiar with how it will work, and will be able to find their way around and deal with any errors they encounter more easily. Most importantly, those consumers will be able to achieve their goals, which should give both consumer and provider a warm, fuzzy feeling.

Consistency Is Key

As PHP developers, we know only too well how difficult it is to use an interface that is inconsistent. The number of manual entries that use the words "needle" and "haystack" with very little correlation between which one should come first in any given situation (and one function where they can be passed in *either* order!) is our reminder of how painful this can be!

In our own applications, we can do better, but it is important to pay attention to the bigger picture and the existing elements of an API while working on building more features. In particular, consideration should be given to how things are named, how the parameters are passed in and returned, and what the expected behavior should be when something unexpected happens.

Consistent and Meaningful Naming

I recently worked with a system that had a function in it called `isSiteAdmin()`. Guess what it returned? Wrong! It actually returned the username of the current user, or `false`. There are plenty of examples of badly named functions in the world, but please protect us from having any more to add to the list. Function names should be meaningful, and they should also be alike. So if there is something called `getCatego` `ries()` available, try to avoid adding a function called `fetchPosts()` or `getAll` `Tags()` unless there's a good reason for the differences. Instead, fit in with the existing convention and call the functions `getPosts()` and `getTags()`.

The same applies to RESTful services, as well as those that contain function names, although it is slightly less of an issue when the clients are following hypermedia links. Look out for consistency in whether collection names are plural or not, for example.

 Case-sensitive or not, make sure your service is absolutely case-consistent throughout.

The naming of parameters is also an area full of traps that are all too easy to fall into —and will annoy your users forever (or at least until you figure out how to release the next version without breaking their existing applications). The way that you name your parameters can give users a clue as to what they should be passing in. For example, a parameter called `user` is rather ambiguous but either `user_id` or `username` would help the user to send more accurate data through to your API.

Naming your parameters with "Hungarian notation" (*https://en.wikipedia.org/wiki/ Hungarian_notation*) is probably a step too far, but aiming more at the verbose than the terse is probably in everyone's interests. If there's a field called `desc` then people will *probably* guess the correct meaning of the abbreviation from the context, but it is clearer to call the parameter `description` or `descending` or whatever it really means.

Common Validation Rules

The benefits of consistency were discussed already, but it is very easy to end up with slightly different validation rules for similar parameters in different settings (for example, whether extra address lines are optional or required between shipping and billing addresses). Also, try to avoid the irritatingly common situation of allowing a particular format of date/time information or telephone number in one place in your API, but not in another.

A good way to ensure that validation is always identical is to always use common functionality, including the built-in features of your framework (this may be documented as form validation but works perfectly well for API parameters too), or the fabulous Filter extension (*http://www.php.net/filter*) in PHP like the example in Example 13-1. The example shows a simple incoming JSON request being decoded and then filtered; if the data is not a valid email address, the value will be `false`.

Example 13-1. The Filter extension in PHP is a great way to validate incoming data

```php
<?php

$clean_data = [];
$incoming = json_decode(
    file_get_contents("php://input"), true
);

$clean_data['email'] = filter_var(
    $incoming['email'],
    FILTER_VALIDATE_EMAIL
);
```

For data types that are specific to your application, you can create a utility class that holds all the validations. In this way, you can add functions that check for particular kinds of data, and then reuse them across your application to ensure consistency.

Predictable Structures

Structure of data is a key characteristic of a service, and a good API design will have it in mind when accepting requests, building responses, and also in the event of any error. APIs that return an array of results should *always* return an array of results. If there's one result, it still needs to be in an array. If there are no results, an empty array should convey this information. Suddenly returning `false`, or showing an item one level up from where it would be in an equivalent endpoint, is confusing, so take care to avoid it.

In most situations, the order in which parameters are provided, either as URL parameters or as part of body content, should not matter. Whether the parameter names or their values are case-sensitive can be made clear in the documentation; it is a challenge to keep these small details correct, particularly across a large API, but it is key and does greatly improve your system.

If an error should occur, it may well be the fault of the user. That said, the API ideally should help the user understand what went wrong and how the user can be better in their use of the API (because otherwise they will log a support ticket that you will have to fix). Error responses should be in a consistent format throughout the API. If a user sees `not-success` in the status code that is returned with his response, he should immediately know how to get the information he needs about what went wrong, in a predictable format.

Predictability is about more than the data formats we saw in Chapter 12, although those are important too. Take care to follow patterns throughout an API regarding what happens when something is created, deleted, or not found so that the user can more quickly align themselves with your ideas and make effective use of your service.

Error Handling in APIs

Errors are a fact of life. Users will enter nonsense into your system, not because they are simpletons (although it does often look that way), but because their expectations and understanding are different from yours. The Internet is a very loosely coupled affair and all kinds of things can and will go wrong at a technical level, once in a while. How your API handles these inevitable situations is a measure of the quality and design of your API, so this section gives some pointers on what to look out for and how to do it well.

Meaningful Error Messages

We all know how frustrating it is to get error messages from systems that say something like "an unknown error has occurred." This gives us absolutely no information at all on how we can coax the application to behave better. Even worse is an application I work with regularly, which will return the error message "Invalid permissions!" in the event that anything at all goes wrong, regardless of whether or not there is a problem with permissions. This leads to people looking in completely the wrong places for solutions and eventually filing very frustrated support tickets.

Error messages should be more than a tidy placeholder that the developer can use to find where in the code she should look when a bug is reported (there is also something to be said in favor of avoiding any copying and pasting of error messages for this reason). The information that an application returns in the event of an error is what lies between the application, the user, and the bug-reporting software. Anyone trying to use an application will have something he is trying to achieve and will be motivated to achieve that goal. If the application can return information about what exactly went wrong, then the user will adjust his attempts and try again, without bothering you. Users tend not to read documentation (developers in particular will usually only read instructions once something isn't working—all engineers do this), so the error information is what forms their experience of the system.

When something goes wrong, answer your user's questions:

- Was a parameter missing or invalid? Was there an unexpected parameter? (A typo can make these two questions arise together very regularly.)
- Was the incoming format invalid? Was it malformed or is it in a format the server does not accept?

- Was a function called that does not exist? (For common mistakes, you might even suggest what the user may have meant.)
- Does the system need to know who the user is before granting access? Or is this user authenticated but with insufficient privileges?

When it exists, give information about which fields are the problem, what is wrong with them, or if something is missing. It is also very helpful to users if you can *collate* the errors as much as possible. Sometimes, errors prevent us from proceeding any further with a request, but if, for example, one of the data fields isn't valid, we could check all the other data fields and return that information all at once. This saves the user from untangling one mistake only to trip straight over the next one, and also shows if the errors are related and could all be fixed in one go.

What to Do When You See Errors

Let us consider our other role in that relationship: that of the consumer of a service. Many of the APIs we work with are not ones we made ourselves, so inevitably we will be encountering some of the behaviors this chapter preaches against. What can we do when this happens? The best approach is to take baby steps.

First, go back to the last known good API call. At the very early stages of working with an API, that means reading the documentation or finding a tutorial to follow, and seeing if you can make any calls at all against this system. Some APIs offer what I call a "heartbeat" method and some offer a status page. Look for something that doesn't need authentication or any complicated parameters to call, and which will let you know that the API is actually working and the problem is at your end. Flickr has a particularly good example of this with their `flickr.test.echo` method (*http://bit.ly/flickr-test-echo*).

Once it has been established that the target API is working, take a look at the call that was being attempted. Does it have any required parameters? Can the call be made in its simplest possible form, passing the smallest possible amount of data with the call? Even once things seem to be improving, it is advisable to approach changes to the API call in small steps, changing data format or adding a parameter, then checking that the response comes back as expected. Just like any kind of debugging, this iterative approach will help to pinpoint which change caused an error to occur.

While these test requests are being made, regardless of which tool is being used, take care to check the headers of the response as well as the body. Status codes, `Content-Type` headers, cache information, and all kinds of other snippets can be visible in the header and give clues about what is happening.

Making Design Decisions for Robustness

Robustness is basically a measure of reassurance; how does the API behave both in good and bad situations? It can be tricky to know which design patterns are the best ones to follow, especially if you are new to APIs. In that situation, good advice would be to stick to the existing standards. These are well-known and understood, and will make it easier for people to integrate with your API or web service. Writing great documentation (see Chapter 14) is key to creating a great API; in general, anything without documentation will not be a good experience for anyone using it.

Finally, always consider what should happen in the event that something goes wrong. How an API behaves in failure cases is how your users will know how robust your service is, so always aim for a consistent and predictable output, regardless of input.

Publishing Your API

Publishing an API is about so much more than just making some endpoints available. In fact, it would be easy to argue that if you're not going to also provide tests and monitoring to ensure the quality of your tools, and excellent documentation so that your users can actually use them, then you could save a lot of time and effort by not setting out to build the API in the first place! Delivering a project is about getting it done, but also creating everything that goes with a successful API. This chapter aims to cover what makes a complete API and show some ways you can deliver this.

Documentation Is Key

Documentation is the magic ingredient that will make your API both useful and usable. Without it, nobody can begin to use or understand the masterpiece you have built. With it, they can build on your offerings and create masterpieces (or at least reliable working software) of their own. Perhaps this chapter should have been the first, not the last, because it does make up a major part of shipping a successful API.

There are many types of documentation, and a great web service probably needs a bit of all of them. The following sections will look at the various kinds of documentation that are useful to accompany a web service and give some suggestions of tools you can use to generate and maintain these.

Overview Documentation

This is the welcoming committee of your API; it gets people over the threshold and gives them confidence that they are about to have a good time. The overview documentation will set the tone of the API and provide some pointers for where to find more detailed information. It could include:

- The main or root endpoint URL

- Information about available formats

- Whether rate limits apply and if results can/should be cached

- Authentication

- Client libraries

- Troubleshooting and further help

In general, overview documentation shows the style and layout of the API and states the protocol(s) that are available. There will probably be some simple examples of requests and responses for common operations to show off the headers and body formats that should be needed. Showing the HTTP for both requests and responses is very useful, because it means that anyone running into problems can fire up a debugger and compare their results with the examples shown.

The overview documentation will also cover how users can identify themselves to the system, if they need to. Many services will allow some public access, while others will ask that users link an API key to their login information on a website. If users need to actually log in, this overview section will cover how to do this, and the method will be the same across all the various parts of the API. This might be a username and password, or an OAuth process to follow, again with clear examples (bonus points if you can manage a real working guest account they can try) showing which credentials go where, where to get any necessary tokens, or how to craft a URL to which they can forward a user.

Information about error states belongs here in the overview, since they will be the same throughout the application. If the error states in your system aren't consistent, then go and read Chapter 13 before reading any further. If you use error codes, provide information about where to find more information about what they mean. If there will be information in the status code or headers, it is helpful to mention it here for any consumers not realizing that they need to look beyond the body text (although this should also contain useful information). Alongside the information about errors, you may also like to include some support information.

Generated API Documentation

Automatically generated documentation can be very helpful if it contains enough information to be useful. The main advantage of this model is that the documentation is maintained inline with the API itself and is therefore more likely to be updated regularly. The jury is still out on whether outdated documentation is actually worse than no documentation at all—personally I think it might be!

In the RPC services, it is common for the entry points to the service to be contained in a single class, and hopefully that class will have inline code documentation. If it does, and especially if this service is for an internal or technical audience, it may be possible to generate API documentation using phpDocumentor (*http://phpdoc.org*) and supply this as a reference to your users. This describes all the methods and parameters in the underlying class, but the PHP SOAP extension, for example, simply provides a very lightweight wrapper, so the generated documentation for the API of that class may well be a very useful artifact to generate and share. Do take care, however, that you're not exposing any undesirable information—for example, implementation details within protected methods.

As an example, we'll use the Event class from Chapter 7 and apply phpDocumentor to it. This tool is very easy to get started with, you can install via PEAR or Composer, but for this example I just grabbed the *phpDocumentor.phar* from the project website and pointed it at the directory with *Event.php* in it. You can see the output in Figure 14-1.

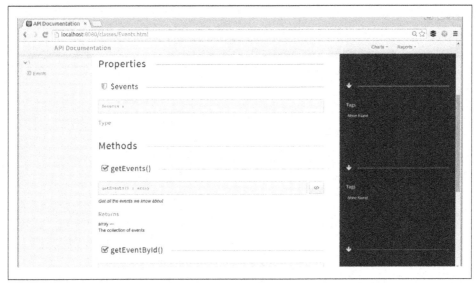

Figure 14-1. API documentation generated by phpDocumentor

This does show which methods can be called and the documentation of both the methods and their respective parameters. It won't be useful in every situation, but phpDocumentor is one of the tools in the proverbial toolbox for offering documentation to users.

Another way of documenting the simple method/parameter outline of SOAP services is to supply a WSDL file, which was covered in Chapter 7.

For a RESTful service it is harder to generate documentation from our PHP code, but existing tools we have in our project can still be used and maintained alongside the API by linking our documentation to our other tools. There are a number of tools that allow you to describe your service using specific formats, and these can integrate with documentation tools. Many of those are also interactive documentation, which we'll move on to look at next.

Interactive Documentation

Some of the best documentation in existence for APIs allows a user to actually try out the request from the documentation page. One great example is Flickr, which offers an API Explorer that allows the user to enter data into the fields and then make the request from the online documentation itself (see Figure 14-2). This allows the user to try the feature as herself or as an anonymous user and set any of the available parameters for a particular method. Flickr gets extra points for technical merit, as they include some handy reference numbers, such as your own user ID and some recent photos uploaded to your account on the same page.

Figure 14-2. Flickr offers interactive API documentation

There are plenty of tools available to help create something similar for another project. One of my preferred approaches is to write a traditional longhand documentation with lots of cURL examples, but instead of just displaying code samples, use hurl.it (*https://www.hurl.it/*) to create textboxes where you can edit and send the cURL requests from the page itself. An example from the Joind.in API documentation is in Figure 14-3 and offers an easy way to show users how to perform a specific request and amend it themselves.

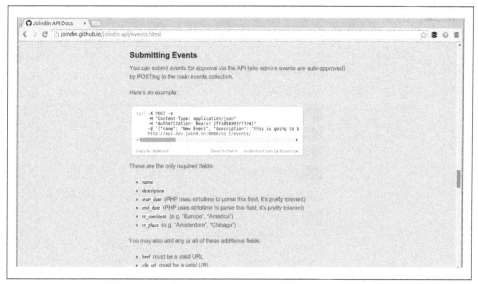

Figure 14-3. Using hurl.it to make a live cURL example in API documentation

Another tool that produces interactive documentation is the I/O Docs (*https://github.com/mashery/iodocs*) tool. It's written in Node.js and the code is open source and available on GitHub, so you can amend it as you need to. You create a configuration file describing how your API can be used, which URLs can be called, what format and parameters to use, and so on. Once you are done, I/O Docs creates a page showing these available actions and parameters as a web form, and allows users to click the alluringly named "Try it!" button to try making a request and viewing the response. This is used by a few online APIs; for example, Klout (*http://devel oper.klout.com/iodocs*) (Twitter metric tools) uses it to document its API, as you can see in Figure 14-4. A tool like this is simple to set up and can be hosted either on your own servers or on a cloud hosting provider such as Heroku.

To use I/O Docs for your own project, you will need to create a configuration file describing the endpoints for your API, which parameters should be sent, which format and authentication should be used, and so on. The project ships with examples for Klout and other well-known APIs, but essentially it's a JSON format.

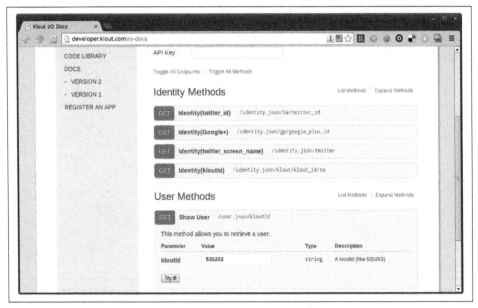

Figure 14-4. Klout uses I/O Docs to create its interactive documentation

API Description Languages

The I/O Docs tool and the idea that you can just describe your API in a known format, then pass that format to an external tool, is an approach that we're seeing more and more often, with hosted or cloud tools as well as offerings for you to host yourself. This approach can be an excellent way of maintaining documentation because it allows you to keep the description files in the same repository as the API source code —so you'd expect to see for any API change a corresponding change in the API description files, therefore helping to keep the two in sync. When you deploy a new version of your API, your build tools can also ship the updated API description file to the tools that use it.

There are a number of competing formats around, and they're all pretty straightforward to work with. In particular you might like to look at API Blueprint (*https:// apiblueprint.org/*), which is a specific markdown format describing an API. In fact, you can create the description and use apiary.io to mock your API to see how it works out before you even build it! There are a number of other tools that integrate with API Blueprint and the list is growing all the time—with your API described, you can expect to find tools to generate documentation, wrapper classes, tests, and various other artifacts from the API Blueprint.

Another markdown-based API description format is RAML (*http://raml.org/index.html*) (it stands for RESTful API Modeling Language), which has various tools associated with it but which is widely used with APIMatic (*https://apimatic.io/*) to create SDK libraries for developers to quickly integrate an API into their project. The markdown formats also serve as a detailed technical specification in their own right, which can make them very useful to produce as part of a project whether your own tooling integrates closely with them or not.

Finally, Swagger (*http://swagger.io*) is also worth a mention although it has rather a different feel as it uses a JSON format so it's more machine-readable than human-readable. Just like the markdown formats though, once you have recorded the metadata about your API, a raft of tools becomes available for users to explore and work with your API.

Automated Testing Tools

In Chapter 10 we saw good ways to store, alter, and replay requests against an API. Many developers find it helpful to keep a library of useful API calls handy and perhaps even to run these as a test suite. In fact we can apply much of what we know about automated testing of websites to our APIs. Techniques you are probably already using such as unit testing are absolutely applicable here. It's also useful to have some integration tests that make HTTP requests against your API and check that everything responds as you'd expect it to; if not, then you know you've made an inadvertent change to your application. There are many, many different tools you could use for this so I've picked two to show you as examples.

 While it might seem a bit odd to have JavaScript tools in a PHP book, the reality is that very many of the best tools in this space are written in node.js! For this section on frisby.js you will need both node.js (*https://nodejs.org/*) and its package manager npm (*https://www.npmjs.com/*) installed on your system.

We'll start with frisby.js (*http://frisbyjs.com*) which, as the name suggests, is a JavaScript tool. Frisby is a lightweight extension to the node.js testing tool jasmine (*https://www.npmjs.com/package/jasmine-node*), which is aimed at making it easier to test API calls and their responses. You can see a snippet of a frisby.js test suite in Example 14-1; you cue up each request and can parse the response to use variables for your next request.

Example 14-1. Use frisby.js to test APIs

```
function testNonexistentUser() {
    frisby.create('Non-existent user')
        .get(baseURL + "/v2.1/users/100100100")
        .expectStatus(404)
        .expectHeader("content-type", "application/json; charset=utf8")
        .expectJSON(["User not found"])
        .toss();
}

function testExistingUser() {
    frisby.create('Existing user')
        .get(baseURL + "/v2.1/users/1")
        .expectStatus(200)
        .expectHeader("content-type", "application/json; charset=utf8")
        .afterJSON(function(allUsers) {
            if (typeof allUsers.users == "object") {
                for (var u in allUsers.users) {
                    var user = allUsers.users[u];
                    datatest.checkUserData(user);
                }
            }
        })
        .toss();
}
```

The example shown checks how the API will respond when a user is requested, both in the case where the user is known to exist, and in the case where the user is known to not exist. To run these tests, we add some configuration for where to find the API endpoint and create a file outlining which functions to call, as shown in Example 14-2.

Example 14-2. Set up frisby.js to run tests (my_spec.js)

```
var apitest  = require('./api_read');

var baseURL;
baseURL = "http://api.dev.joind.in";

apitest.init(baseURL);
apitest.testNonexistentUser();
apitest.testExistingUser();
```

Use the installation instructions on frisbyjs.com to get frisby installed and then you can run this example yourself. The output is pretty much as you'd expect, just a few lines reporting the outcome:

```
$ jasmine-node my_spec.js
..

Finished in 0.111 seconds
2 tests, 23 assertions, 0 failures, 0 skipped
```

This also makes it very easy to include in a build process. API tests, like integration tests, can't be run on a codebase until it is deployed and can be reached via HTTP. I have the test runs set up as Jenkins jobs so that it is super-easy to run the tests against either the test or live platforms (nondestructive tests only!) when you have just deployed a new version. It is also well worth the investment of time to make these tests trivially easy to run on development platforms so that developers can very easily verify they haven't accidentally broken anything—as well as testing their own new tests alongside their features of course.

A similar approach might be to create a new PHPUnit test suite to include in your application and have it just make API calls and check the responses (remember to check what happens in the failure case as well), using a library such as Guzzle that has been used elsewhere in the book. One advantage of this is that you probably already have PHPUnit in use in your project for unit tests, so it saves learning another tool for other tests such as API or functional integration tests.

Another alternative for API testing is to use a hosted tool. For this example, I've chosen Runscope (*https://www.runscope.com*), as I find it very easy to get started and it tells me very clearly exactly what is wrong if something does break. The way it works is that you create some tests, which can be whole sequences of API requests, with variables fetched and stored between them, and save them. Runscope will then allow you to use this interface to run the tests, but can also run them periodically from a variety of locations around the world, allowing you to check your performance from a selection of geographical regions.

I've set up a test that just creates a user and then fetches the new record; you can see the configuration in Figure 14-5. I have it set to run automatically and email me if there are any failures; I only visit the site to add more tests or to investigate in the event of a failure.

Having automated API testing, whether on your own build servers or from another service, is really valuable to make sure that there are no regressions, bad data, or other issues cropping up in your application. You can also use standard monitoring and health-check tools to make sure that your APIs are as available as they should be, or to alert you if there are any problems.

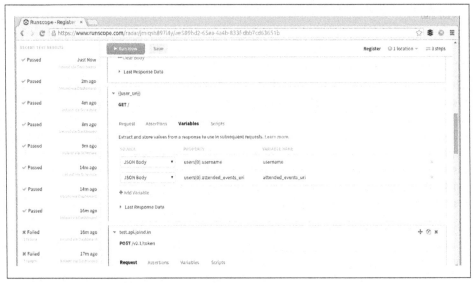

Figure 14-5. Configuring a Runscope test

Tutorials and the Wider Ecosystem

Documentation is about so much more than lists of accessible functionality. It is about showing how the API actually solves problems, and how it looks when it is used in the real world. A common criticism of software library documentation is that, while each function is documented, it can be very hard to know which function you want to use. Giving practical tutorial examples is really useful, even when they are not exactly what a user was looking for. In creating these tutorials you have essentially two choices: write them yourself, or keep an eye out and encourage your community to contribute.

When writing tutorials, there are some key points that can help create useful, readable additions to your existing documentation. Focus in each tutorial on just one particular skill or technique (for example, I wrote a very specific blog post (*http://bit.ly/ jira-rest-api*) for interacting with JIRA's API). If you need to refer to other skills, then link out to documentation on doing that (how to set up your SSH keys, how to configure your editor, etc.). Sometimes this means that writing one tutorial can mean you end up writing a miniseries with three or four articles in it to produce the content that works as a whole. Splitting things up into focused chunks both allows the user to more easily find what they need but also keeps the articles short enough that an average user stands a chance of getting to the end. The other thing to remember is that more information is always helpful. So spell it out with detailed examples, full code samples (with syntax highlighting), screenshots, and plenty of subheadings to break up long reams of text. It's hard to know which small detail a user might have missed; and more information helps them to put the clues together and achieve their goals.

Make sure your users know where they can go for support; then go and find where they actually *ask* for help. While you may set up user forums to help people with their queries and make those details public so that other people can find answers to common questions, users often don't follow the paths you set for them. Sometimes it is necessary to "pave the cowpaths" and follow where they lead. To this end, set up a search alert for your product or application name with a search engine, and make sure that when questions do pop up in other places (such as StackOverflow (*http:// stackoverflow.com*)), someone is able to respond.

Having documentation outside of your own control is a very positive thing, although it can feel a little frightening at first. Users are the word of mouth that spread influence, and often they can become your biggest advocates and very effectively help one another. Welcome those users who contribute to the wider project and credit them where you can; documentation from any angle is a resource that's valuable to any project and it's vital for anything public. It is referred to as the "ecosystem" because it's the world your application exists in.

A Guide to Common Status Codes

This section outlines some of the most common status codes in use in HTTP APIs, their meaning, and some notes about when they can be used.

Code	Meaning	Notes
100	Continue	For a large request, a client can send just the headers and `Expect: 100-continue` as an additional header. If the 100 status is received in response, the client can then send the request as normal. Think of it as "go ahead"—in fact, many libraries will handle this for you and make the second request without further prompting.
200	OK	This is good news; everything worked as expected.
201	Created	A new resource was created. This is often accompanied by a `Location` header or a representation of the new resource in the body of the request.
202	Accepted	This is useful if something is taken to be actioned later, such as being placed on a queue for asynchronous processing.
204	No Content	The request was successful, but there is nothing to return. Perhaps this is the result of a `DELETE` request.
301	Moved Permanently	The content is at a new location, and this is a permanent change. Links to the old URL must be updated, and this change will often be cached for long periods.
302	Found	This is much like a 200, but the content was not at the location specified. Usually this is seen when an application uses rewrite rules.

Code	Meaning	Notes
304	Not Modified	This is sent in response to a request that included information such as an `ETag` or `Last-Modified`, which indicates that the resource is cached and specifies which version the client has. This status code means "use the one you have" and is useful to avoid repeatedly transferring large representations that don't change.
400	Bad Request	This is the general "something went wrong" status. Sometimes there may be no more detail to offer; at other times, you may choose not to transmit anything more.
401	Unauthorized	Credentials are needed in order to access this resource.
403	Forbidden	This contrasts with `401` and means that any credentials given were not sufficient to access this resource.
404	Not Found	A request was made for something the server doesn't have or doesn't know how to provide. Alternatively, a request was made for a resource that isn't available to this user and the 404 doesn't leak information about the potential existence of such a resource.
405	Method Not Allowed	The verb used to access this URL isn't supported—this is useful if, for example, you don't allow updates to a resource but a `PUT` request was received.
406	Not Acceptable	The server cannot generate a response in accordance with the `Accept` headers that came with the request.
409	Conflict	There is a mismatch between versions of resources, such as an incoming update when the resource has changed in the meantime.
410	Gone	A resource did exist, but doesn't any more. Many services will simply return a `404` here, or a `409` may also be appropriate, particularly if something is trying to perform an update on the resource.
415	Unsupported Media Type	The media type specified in the `Content-Type` header isn't understood by this server.
429	Too Many Requests	Usually used with rate-limiting schemes, although Twitter uses `420` "Enhance Your Calm" for this purpose.
500	Internal Server Error	An unhandled error occurred, and is the fault of the server rather than the client. In PHP applications, PHP has usually segfaulted, leaving the web server unable to return any useful information.
501	Not Implemented	The server can't handle this request; it may also indicate that a documented feature is currently still under construction.
502	Bad Gateway	This indicates that a proxy server of some sort has failed, such as a load balancer.

Code	Meaning	Notes
503	Service Unavailable	This is usually seen when a server is temporarily offline, such as during a planned maintenance window. Often, it really means "try again later" but it also discourages caching, and is particularly useful to stop search engines from finding and caching your temporary holding page.

For a full list of status codes, there is an excellent reference on Wikipedia (*http://bit.ly/wiki-status-codes*).

Common HTTP Headers

Here we look at a series of often-used headers, whether they are request or response headers, and how they can be used.

Header	Request	Response	Notes
Accept	yes		This shows the formats, with an indication of preference, that the requesting client can understand. Closely related are the additional headers `Accept-Charset`, `Accept-Encoding`, and `Accept-Language`.
Authorization	yes		This is free-form information to prove a user's identity. This is used in basic authentication, digest authentication, OAuth, and so on; each has their own format of exactly what goes in the header.
Cookie	yes		Cookies are key/value pairs sent with each request, separated by a semicolon. This is the sister header to `Set-Cookie`.
Content-Length	yes	yes	Any request or response with body content should also have the `Content-Length` in bytes in the header; often your HTTP library will calculate this for you.
Content-Type	yes	yes	Any request or response with body content should include the `Content-Type` header to provide information about the format of that body content. As with the Accept headers, `Content-Encoding` and `Content-Language` may also be sent to give information about the format of the content.
ETag		yes	This is an identifier for the version of the resource that is being returned. If the client caches the resource, this information can be used with `If-None-Match` to work out whether a resource has been updated or if the previous version can be used.

Header	Request	Response	Notes
If-Modified-Since and If-None-Match	yes		This informs the server that there is a cached copy of this resource and allows the server to return a 304 status code if that resource is still valid.
Last-Modified		yes	This provides information about when this resource was last updated; the client can use this to check if it has the most recent version of the resource upon subsequent requests.
Location		yes	This provides information about a location and is used either with 300-series status codes when redirecting, or with 201/202 to give information about the location of a new resource.
Set-Cookie		yes	This sends cookies to be stored on the client and sent back in a `Cookie` header with later requests.
User-Agent	yes		This provides information about the client software making the request.

Index

cURL
    and debug output, 118-120
    demonstrating Accept header with, 33
    graphical alternatives to, 100
curl command, 88
cURL command-line tool, 6-10
curl_setopt() function, 13
custom headers, 38

D

data structures, 141
data types, for services, 131
debugging (see maintainable web services)
default values, for APIs, 137
DELETE verb, 23, 88
documentation
    and API description languages, 150
    automatically generated, 146-148
    for APIs, 145-149
    interactive, 148
    overview type, 145
    tutorials, 154
DOM, 55
dumpcap command, 104

E

ecosystem, documentation and, 155
error handling
    in APIs, 142
    what to do when you see errors, 143
    with Exception class, 123-126
error logging
    effective techniques for, 120-123
    libraries for, 121
    Monolog for, 122
error messages, meaningful, 142
errors, user, 141
error_log() function, 120
ETag header, 38
Exception class, 123-126
exception handlers, 81
exit() function, 118

F

FireBug, 10
Firefox, 10, 100
Flickr
    API using XML, 58-61

interactive API documentation, 148
Formatter class, 115
frisby.js, 151

G

generated documentation, 146-148
GET requests
    examples, 12-14
    for fetching representations of resources, 84-87
    making, 19
    serving, 17
gists, 51
GitHub, 92-94, 130
Guzzle, 12, 14, 111

H

HAL (Hypertext Application Language), 131
headers, 27-39
    Accept, 30-34
    and HTTP Basic authentication, 35
    and HTTP Digest authentication, 36
    and OAuth, 36
    Authorization, 34-37
    caching, 37
    common, 161
    Content-Type, 30
    custom, 38
    for content negotiation, 30-34
    request, 28
    response, 28
    User-Agent, 29
HTML, data presentation with, 129
HTTP, 1-15
    and browser tools, 10
    clients and servers, 4
    command-line, 6-10
    making requests, 5-15
    request handling with PHP, 12-15
    tools (see HTTP tools)
    verbs (see HTTP verbs)
HTTP Basic authentication, 35
HTTP Digest authentication, 36
HTTP headers (see headers)
HTTP tools, 97-112
    easy command-line JSON, 98
    for editing network settings, 108
    for inspecting traffic, 107-111
    for sharing sessions, 107

SugarCRM, 66
Swagger, 151

T

testing, automated tools for, 151-153
throttling traffic, 110
tools (see HTTP tools)
TravisCI, 92
tunneling, ngrok for, 105-106
tutorials, 154

U

Uniform Resource Identifier (URI), 69
URLs, RESTful, 76
user forums, 155
User-Agent header, 29
users, considering needs of, 127

V

vagrant ssh command, 104
validation rules, consistency of, 140
Varnish, 38
verbs (see HTTP verbs)
versioning, 134

W

webhooks, 91-96
    GitHubs, 92-94
    publishing your own, 94
wildcards, 31
Wireshark, 97, 101-105
wishlist (RESTful example service), 79-81
WSDL (Web Service Description Language), 66
    generating a file from PHP, 70-72
    PHP client and server with, 72

X

XML, 53-61
    consuming XML APIs, 58-61
    creating simple document, 55-58
    Flickr's XML API, 58-61
    in PHP, 55-58
    parsing, 58
    when to choose, 54
XMLParser, 55
XMLReader, 55
XMLWriter, 55

About the Author

Lorna Jane Mitchell is an independent web development consultant, specializing in PHP and APIs in particular. With over 10 years of PHP development experience across a wide variety of industries, Lorna learned many lessons the hard way and always has a story to tell. Lorna is also an experienced trainer, offering training to private clients around the world, and teaching public courses. A prolific writer, Lorna writes for a number of publications, and frequently for her own blog (*http://lorna jane.net*).

Colophon

The animal on the cover of *PHP Web Services* is an alpine accentor (*Prunella collaris*). This bird inhabits the mountain ranges of southern Europe, Asia, and Lebanon, favoring heights above 2,000 meters; it has actually been spotted near the top of Mount Everest at nearly 8,000 meters.

Alpine accentors are drab in color, with a gray head and breast, brown-streaked back, and reddish-brown spotted underparts. They are typically 15–17 centimeters long, weighing up to 35 grams. Sharp, pointed bills help them sustain their diet of ground-dwelling insects, spiders, earthworms, and plant seeds.

They are noted for their unconventional breeding systems: they mate in polygynandrous groups, usually consisting of up to four males and four females, which often produces mixed paternity within broods. Females build nests sheltered by bushes or rock crevices and lay approximately four sky-blue eggs. Males will sometimes help feed nestlings, if they have mated with the female and thereby assume paternity. Accentors may have two to three broods per year.

The cover image is from Wood's *Animate Creation*. The cover font is Adobe ITC Garamond. The text font is Adobe Minion Pro; the heading font is Adobe Myriad Condensed; and the code font is Dalton Maag's Ubuntu Mono.

9 781491 933091